LINES ACROSS LINCOLNSHIRE

Discovering Routes, Banks & Boundaries

Jon Fox

ABOVE: **landscape lines from the Lincoln Edge, Bracebridge Heath**

First published in 2018 by Green Plover Books

21 Cambridge Avenue, Lincoln, LN1 1LS

www.greenploverbooks.co.uk

Text and photographs by Jon Fox

Dedication: To Lois and to my parents, Alan and Valerie

ISBN: 978-0-9932696-1-5

Book design by Jon Fox. Timelines and map artwork by David Would with base map assistance from Adam Daubney

Printed by L.E.G.O. S.p.A., Vicenza, Italy

FSC
MIX
Paper from
responsible sources
FSC® C023419
www.fsc.org

RIGHT: **former peat trackway, Crowle Moor**

Contents

Timelines: a brief chronology of Lincolnshire's landscape...

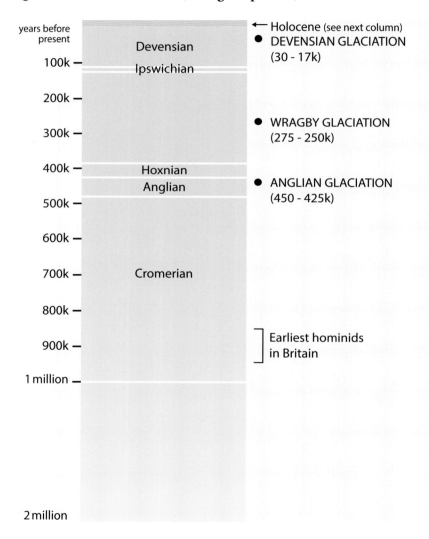

GEOLOGICAL PERIODS

years before present (millions)

Tertiary

← Quaternary (see next column)

100 —

Cretaceous

Lincolnshire's bedrock laid down

Jurassic

200 —

Triassic

300 —

400 —

500 —

600 —

4,600

Age of the Earth

QUATERNARY STAGES (Ice Age to present)

years before present

Devensian

← Holocene (see next column)
● DEVENSIAN GLACIATION (30 - 17k)

100k —

Ipswichian

200k —

● WRAGBY GLACIATION (275 - 250k)

300k —

400k —

Hoxnian

Anglian

● ANGLIAN GLACIATION (450 - 425k)

500k —

600k —

700k —

Cromerian

800k —

900k —

Earliest hominids in Britain

1 million —

2 million

4

HOLOCENE (Our own geological epoch)

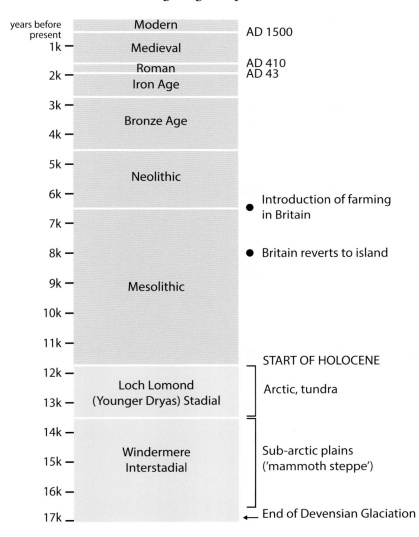

MODERN

Postwar	1945 - 1970s
World War II	1939 - 1945
Interwar	1918 - 1939
World War I	1914 - 1918
Edwardian	1901 - 1910
Victorian	1837 - 1901
Georgian & Regency	1714 - 1837
Stuart	1603 - 1714
Tudor	1485 - 1603

MEDIEVAL

Norman and Plantagenet	1066 - 1485
Anglo-Saxon	410 - 1066
Anglo-Danish (Late Anglo-Saxon)	850 - 1066
Middle Anglo-Saxon	650 - 850
Early Anglo-Saxon	410 - 650
Romano-British	AD 43 - 410

PREHISTORIC

Iron Age		800 BC - AD 43
Bronze Age	4,500 - 2,800 BP	2,500 - 800 BC
Neolithic	6,500 - 4,500 BP	4,500 - 2,500 BC
Mesolithic	11,700 - 6,500 BP	9,700 - 4,500 BC
Palaeolithic	c. 1 m - 11,700 BP	c. 1 m - 9,700 BC

(BP = years before present)

5

INTRODUCTION

Lines are a fundamental element in most landscapes, and the countryside of Lincolnshire is perhaps defined more than most by linearity. The parallel lines of intensive arable farming – tractor marks and cultivation rows – now dominate much of the county. When combined with level horizons, ruler-straight drains and droves in the former wetlands, the result is a strikingly linear countryside unequalled in England outside the Fens. In places, this is a landscape reduced to straight lines, almost to mathematical abstraction.

However, not all of Lincolnshire exhibits extreme rectilinearity. Firstly, there are the uplands, where the natural topography bends the lines of farming into curves and waves, above all in the chalk Wolds with their undulating expanses and convex hillsides. And, considered more closely, agriculture has its own curves too, independent of relief. Even the largest Fenland fields have an edge where farm machinery must turn when undertaking rolling, harrowing, drilling or crop applications, thereby adding the circle to the linear geometry of the modern farmed landscape.

Arable operations produce temporary lines, but the boundaries of fields in Lincolnshire are mostly bequeathed from the past and often depart from rectangular or square form to impose their own irregularities on the farmed present. Added to this in varying degrees and patterns are the other lines of the inherited countryside, including watercourses, paths, lanes, hedges and woods, as well as the parks and plantations of country estates. Successive transport developments from the 17th century onwards then cut across the farmed countryside with their own lines, including canals and railways, some of which have now moved into the realm of archaeology through closure or taken on new recreational uses. The last century added telegraph wires, pylons, motorways and various military lines from two World Wars.

The more one looks at the Lincolnshire landscape, the more it becomes clear that most of the lines visible today are the product of the human past, either as physically surviving historical features, or as 'continuities' where old alignments have been reused without necessarily preserving their original fabric or purpose. Sea banks are a good example, ranging from upstanding earthworks to 'ghost' lines marked only by paths, tracks or field boundaries. Thus, with the possible exception of the newest lands around the Wash, reclaimed from saltmarsh in the 1970s, almost all of Lincolnshire's landscape is a complex patchwork of new and reused lines from history.

Broadly, the main categories of man-made lines in the landscape of Lincolnshire are: routes for movement; field boundaries and drainage works, including 'ridge and furrow'; embankments for flood defence and reclamation; territorial or defensive lines; and the edges created by zoned activities including industry and forestry. Many of these have a long pedigree stretching back into prehistory and, in the case of pathways,

FACING PAGE: **farmland on chalk plateau, Lincolnshire Wolds**

probably into the Ice Age. The discovery of Cromerian age footprints on the East Anglian coast has pushed back known human presence in Britain to approaching a million years, well before the Anglian glaciation. Lincolnshire has Palaeolithic artefacts such as flint tools, but successive glacial advances appear to have obliterated any linear features older than the Mesolithic. With the latter period, defined pathways almost certainly emerged in the forests, while the pollen record suggests savannah-like zones were being created and maintained for hunting in the Kesteven Uplands. Even so, it would be pushing the evidence too far to propose continuities with modern routes or the boundaries of woodland or heath today.

The oldest human lines that can still be traced with certainty in the Lincolnshire landscape probably therefore date to later prehistory, after the introduction of farming. From the four millennia after 4,500 BC, archaeology gives us the physical remains of timber causeways in the Fens and Humberhead Levels and a variety of linear crop marks. The latter include complex field systems along the Kesteven Fen Edge and linear features crossing the Lincoln Heath and Cliff that probably represent trackways and/or the boundaries of Iron Age farming territories.

Uncertainty still surrounds prehistoric transport routes, however. Long-distance movement across Neolithic Britain is clearly evidenced by pan-British festivities at Stonehenge and the archaeological distribution of traded

TOP LEFT: **Trent Valley heathland.** Natural habitat or early human landscape?

LEFT: **potato ridges in the silt Fens.** Farmed landscape as linear geometry.

products such as stone axeheads and flint, all pointing to an established 'national' transport network by this time. Yet the details remain hazy. Even the 'Jurassic Way', postulated in the 1930s and 40s as a trackway between Yorkshire and Somerset along the limestone uplands, tidily linking the then known prehistoric sites, is now seen by scholars more as a movement corridor than a single route. That said, the intensively farmed countryside of Iron Age Lincolnshire suggests that roads including Middle Street and Pottergate became well-defined and possibly even enclosed against straying livestock well before the Romans arrived.

Turning to the Romans, they are still widely regarded as the ultimate creators of straight lines in the landscape. Their rule-like roads of military conquest are undeniably impressive as works of surveying and construction. However, the appeal of the Roman *imperium* to Britain's elite from the Renaissance onwards has tended to obscure native, pre-Roman advances in engineering, including roads, as well as fuelling the misattribution of lines from other historical periods. Anything in Lincolnshire named Roman Bank is almost certainly not so! Even today, features such as the Car Dyke and the Fossdyke Canal are often boldly asserted as Roman in origin, despite not being definitively proven as such. Indeed, an Anglo-Danish date has recently been suggested for the latter canal.

The main categories of human lines continually reappear in new guises throughout Lincolnshire's long history, reflecting successive changes in

RIGHT: **Bloxholm Lane, Lincoln Heath**. Prehistoric route or Roman road?

social organisation, land use and technology. Sometimes there is continuity even through periods of profound landscape change, as seen where Medieval field boundaries survived the enclosure process. Remarkably, new research indicates that some field alignments and possibly even boundaries may date back to the Romano-British period, even in areas like Lincolnshire where Medieval open fields developed and many parish layouts were later redrawn by Parliamentary enclosure. Conversely, some lines were completely novel, like the railways, even if these sometimes shadowed older features like river embankments and drains.

Perhaps distinct as a category are lines in the landscape created primarily for aesthetic purposes, as seen in country house parks. Here, we encounter both formal geometry in the avenues and 'starburst' patterns of the late 1600s, and more naturalistic designs with linear elements such as serpentine lakes and blocks of woodland, as epitomised by 'Capability' Brown's English Landscape Style. These are perhaps the first lines in the countryside created as conscious art, though some see Neolithic ritual landscapes, with their complex monuments and alignments, as expressions of creativity. Such landscapes might have existed in Lincolnshire on the chalk Wolds.

Ultimately, most human lines reflect the natural landscape and its underlying patterns from geology and ecology. Even the famed disregard of natural features by Roman roads has been overstated – choice of route and course adjustments were in fact made in response to topography. Obviously, Nature had its own lines in the landscape millions of years before humans evolved, including linear landforms, watercourses and coastlines. The vector force of gravity drove Lincolnshire's geological history of sedimentary deposition and the subsequent weathering of rocks by wind and water. Together with the more episodic and dramatic earth processes of tectonic uplift and glaciation, this has given the county its simple but striking topography of alternate uplands and lowlands. These form natural bands of landscape character running broadly north-south, and underpin much in the modern landscape from natural drainage to the strongly linear patterns of Medieval settlement still present today. The upland escarpments are particularly notable as linear organising features, their spring lines manifested in long lines of 'cliff' villages. Similar settlement lines occur along river valleys, wetland edges and former coastlines.

Natural topography has strongly influenced if not determined most human activity in the landscape from farming to transport, the latter making use of Lincolnshire's uplands and river gaps from prehistory into modern times. The Lincoln Gap even attracted Britain's first 'East Coast' main line railway in the 1840s, before a more direct route was blasted through the Kesteven Uplands between Peterborough and Grantham.

Coastlines past and present have added their own linearities to Lincolnshire's landscape, both natural and human. Several former coastlines can still be traced, including relict sea cliffs from 125,000 years ago overlooking the Marsh and Fens. Coastal human lines include sea banks and their accompanying settlements, holiday resorts, wartime defences and the modern port and industrial complexes along the Humber Bank.

FACING PAGE: **fields and track, Walesby**

12

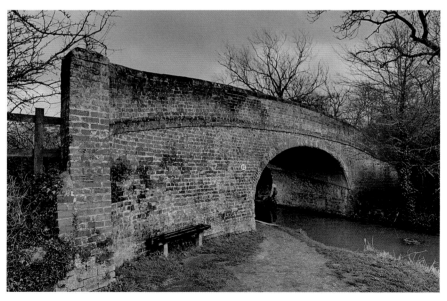

Most man-made lines were constructed with deliberate intent, albeit that early trackways may have emerged more by repeated use than conscious planning. However, a further set of human lines results from 'zonal' activity, where a physical or ecological boundary occurs between the activity and adjoining land. Woodland plantations are an obvious example, with defined edges that form visible lines in the landscape. Few if any vegetational boundaries are natural; nature mostly has gradual transitions or 'ecotones'. Other historic activities creating bounded zones include peat digging, salt making, quarrying and hunting by the elite. In some cases there is a constructed boundary too, such as the woodbank around Medieval woods or fencing around industrial sites, usually to emphasise ownership and/or to prevent unwanted entry. Some boundaries were primarily to keep animals in, such as most hedges and the 'pale' around Medieval deer parks, though the exclusion of people and livestock was also a frequent objective. Like most aspects of the human landscape, lines often have a

Historical conjunctions and intersects on lines (CLOCKWISE FROM TOP LEFT):

Beech trees from the 18th century along a probable Medieval or earlier track, Warren Lane, Lincoln Heath

Anglo-Saxon fen bank (probably pre-850) with modern tarmac and road signage, Quadring, Fens

Humber Bridge (opened 1981) crossing the River Humber (pre-Anglian river and principal Danish route into Anglo-Saxon England)

Longmoor Lane (possible prehistoric trackway) crossing the Grantham Canal (opened 1797), Woolsthorpe / Denton

legal significance relating to ownership and access rights, often embodying underlying social relationships. Norman Forest Law is an early example, though here the boundaries were not necessarily marked physically on the ground.

In the 20th century, state intervention increased dramatically in a new age of technological lines, encompassing both peace time and war. Governments planned and built major infrastructure networks including the National Grid, new roads for the expansion of motorised transport, and numerous military airfields and other lines of defence. Conversely, public policy and regulation also became increasingly important in controlling development and protecting wildlife in the countryside. These interventions are widely manifested in the landscape as 'policy zones' with defined boundaries, such as AONBs, SSSIs, nature reserves, green corridors and planned allocations for open countryside and development. Wildlife strips, replanted hedges and woodland belts are new linear features of farmland since the 1980s.

Today, we are the inheritors of a fascinating composite of landscape lines from every period from prehistoric to modern, continually crossing and re-crossing each other from different points in history. Perhaps more than any other aspect of the landscape, they express the beliefs, aspirations and fears of each generation. Hopefully, they can stimulate us to consider our own contribution to the ongoing story of Lincolnshire's landscape.

...and the space between the lines?

When considering the lines, don't forget the landscape in between....

1 : ESCARPMENTS
Natural Lines from Geology

Even a quick glance at a geology map of Lincolnshire shows that the county's underlying structure is one of parallel bands of rock running in a broadly north-south direction (see map on page 28). A journey from east to west from the River Trent to the North Sea coastline thus traverses a succession of linear geological formations, each of which is manifested as a distinct landscape character area – Vale of Trent, Lincoln Cliff, Lindsey Vale, Wolds and Lindsey Marsh. Further south, the pattern is simpler – the Fenland basin forming a broader band between the Kesteven Uplands and the chalk edge in Norfolk – but essentially the same (Fox, 2015).

Closer inspection reveals that the same linearity and orientation are expressed within the character areas too, both in natural landforms and associated patterns of human settlement and land use. This is seen most clearly in the escarpments or scarps formed by the harder rocks, including limestones, ironstones and sandstones. This chapter focuses on escarpments as natural linear features, exploring their distinctive contribution to the Lincolnshire landscape. It traces the relationship between escarpments and people, including their importance as prehistoric 'ways' and in shaping village settlement, parish and field patterns. The role of escarpments

FACING PAGE: **Wolds escarpment north of Claxby**

as industrial landscapes is also noted, as they provided access to ironstones that were mined and quarried commercially until the 1970s.

Escarpments in Lincolnshire: origins and location

Most of Lincolnshire's underlying geology or bedrock – mudstones, ironstones, limestones and chalk – was laid down in estuarial or marine conditions in the Mesozoic era, encompassing Triassic, Jurassic and Cretaceous sediments dating from 200 to 65 million years ago. By contrast, the Tertiary period was one of terrestrial erosion in the context of the earth movements that built the Alps, which also raised and tilted the rocks along a roughly north-south axis. Tentatively, an uplifted surface of Cretaceous chalk stretching over the whole county was gradually stripped away during Tertiary times to reveal the older rocks beneath, leaving only the chalk Wolds of east Lincolnshire (Swinnerton & Kent, 1976).

Over time, the harder and softer strata developed into uplands and lowlands respectively, the precursors of those seen today. The tilting of the strata gave the upland belts a characteristic 'cuesta' profile, each with a steep, west-facing escarpment or scarp and a much gentler dip slope declining gradually eastwards.

By the start of the Quaternary period, therefore, and perhaps some time before, a recognisable precursor topography of modern Lincolnshire had probably emerged, with the twin upland belts of the Jurassic Oolites and Wolds and a North Sea coastline somewhere to the east, the latter moving in response to the glacial cycle (see Chapter 3). Successive glaciations then eroded and smoothed the uplands further whilst also gouging the clay lowlands into vales and the Fen Basin. Over geological time, terrestrial weathering of the scarps caused them to recede eastwards, though this process is generally too slow to have had a major effect on the human landscape.

Today, there are five main escarpments in Lincolnshire, as shown on the map on page 28. The landscapes and history of each is explored in turn.

Lincolnshire's bedrock consists almost entirely of sedimentary rocks laid down in coastal and marine conditions. The Triassic Mercia Mudstone, Lincolnshire's oldest rock, is thought to have been deposited as mudflats on a vast coastal plain in a very hot climate when Britain lay much closer to the Equator and was still part of the Pangaea supercontinent. Subsequently, in the Jurassic and Cretaceous periods, Lincolnshire was mostly submerged as part of a shallow tropical sea which stretched east to Russia, when the county's oolitic limestones and chalk were deposited. However, other rocks of this time – ironstones, sandstones and mudstones – were deposited in coastal swamps and lagoons, indicating a complex series of marine advances and retreats. In the subsequent Tertiary period, Lincolnshire was part of land north-east of the sea which laid down the London Clay, and experienced tectonic uplift and terrestrial erosion.

ABOVE: **Spilsby Sandstone exposure near Stenigot, Wolds**

FACING PAGE: **Trent Cliff seen across the River Trent from Garthorpe**

The Liassic escarpments (1): Vale of Trent & Trent Cliff

Lincolnshire has a toehold on the Mercia Mudstone along the Trent Valley and on the 'islands' of the Isle of Axholme, but the main escarpment of this Triassic formation lies several miles to the west in Nottinghamshire. The first cuesta escarpment encountered when travelling eastwards in Lincolnshire is therefore that of the Early Jurassic or Liassic rocks which appear just east of the River Trent. The mudstones here contain a number of harder limestone beds which create generally subdued and discontinuous scarp features within the Vale of Trent. It has to be said that these are mostly of very limited landscape impact in visual and other terms, though there are exceptions such as Lincoln Hill in the southern Vale, which provides a notable hilltop setting for the village of Dry Doddington.

Much more emphatic is Trent Cliff, where the Liassic limestones are augmented by the Frodingham Ironstone, producing a striking escarpment overlooking the Trent for several miles as the river approaches and merges into the Humber. Trent Cliff provides the setting for several settlements of pre-Conquest origin, including Flixborough, Burton-upon-Stather, Alkborough and Whitton, while the staithes at Flixborough and Burton had Medieval precursors as the river's trade developed. Behind the scarp, the ironstone forms a bench of land declining to the next escarpment eastwards, the Lincoln Edge, and has been used locally as a building stone in the villages. The Lower Lias escarpment continues southwards in more subdued form as far as Scotter, via Frodingham, Yaddlethorpe and Messingham. Iron ore deposits associated with the ironstone helped fuel Scunthorpe's industrial growth as an iron and steel boomtown in the 19th century, its suburbs ultimately spilling over the low escarpment as they engulfed the old clifftop villages.

The Liassic escarpments (2): Marlstone

The next escarpment eastwards is formed by another Liassic 'ironstone', known as the Marlstone Rock Formation – loosely, Marlstone – which outcrops in Lincolnshire principally in the Grantham area. North of Lincoln, the Marlstone beds are present but thin and produce only a

FACING PAGE: **Marlstone scarp near Hough-on-the-Hill**

TOP RIGHT: **mixed Marlstone and Oolite masonry, Caythorpe**

relatively minor 'step' feature at the foot of the Lincoln Edge. Southwards from Leadenham, though, the Marlstone increases in thickness to create its own cuesta with a western escarpment and dip slope. The scarp runs roughly parallel to the Lincoln Edge, pushing south-west into Leicestershire near Belvoir Castle, where it becomes a formidable rampart overlooking the Vale of Belvoir and reaches well over 500 ft (150 m) in altitude. Within Lincolnshire, it is lower and more broken by streams, including the River Witham. Nevertheless, it is a significant landscape feature, with hilltop villages including Leadenham, Fulbeck, Caythorpe, Hough-on-the-Hill, Great Gonerby and Barrowby.

The Marlstone has yielded building stone historically – a rich, orange-brown, sandy limestone seen widely in churches and older vernacular buildings

The Oolitic Limestones or Oolites of the Middle Jurassic are named after the tiny, spheroidal particles called 'ooliths' that make up many of the limestones, loosely resembling fish roe. Several limestones in this formation have been extracted as fine building stones, including the famous 'freestones' of the Lincolnshire Limestone quarried at Ancaster, Barnack (Northants), Clipsham (Rutland), Lincoln and elsewhere. Middle Jurassic limestones are seen in older buildings throughout Lincolnshire's Oolite belt from Stamford to the Humber, as here at **Harlaxton Manor** (LEFT) and were also transported further afield for churches and other important buildings due to their endurance, carvability and aesthetic qualities.

northwards from the Leicestershire Wolds to Caythorpe and occasionally north of Lincoln. Iron-rich beds within the Marlstone have also been extensively mined as ore. There is an important archaeology commencing in the 1790s around Belvoir that includes former mineral 'tramways' and inclines linking to the nearby Grantham Canal (Hewlett, 1935). Further opencast mines were developed between Fulbeck and Honington after the opening of the branch railway from Lincoln in the 1860s (Tonks, 1991).

The cultural significance of the Marlstone escarpment in earlier times is probably underestimated. Its interrupted form in Lincolnshire may have discouraged its use by prehistoric travellers as a long-distance route, but the prominent hilltops and wide vistas almost certainly attracted people. Loveden Hill is particularly notable for its archaeology, including one

of England's largest Anglo-Saxon cemeteries. The numerous burial urns and grave goods found at the site are now housed at The Collection in Lincoln. The hill is also thought to have been the meeting place for the Loveden wapentake in the Anglo-Saxon period and may have held religious or territorial significance going back into prehistoric times.

The Lincoln Edge: Oolites, Jurassic Way & cliff villages

The Lincoln Edge is Lincolnshire's longest escarpment by far, running for over 60 miles (97 km) from Denton to Winteringham. Structurally, it extends even further, running southwards into Rutland and briefly north of the Humber too. Apart from short river gaps at Grantham, Ancaster and

Lincoln Edge or Lincoln Cliff? In Lincolnshire, the term 'cliff' can be applied to any steep slope that forms a linear feature in the landscape. South of Lincoln, the Lincoln Edge is often referred to alternatively as the Lincoln Cliff, and its settlements are known locally as the Cliff Villages. In Lindsey, by comparison, the name Lincoln Cliff has traditionally been used for the entire limestone ridge of the Oolites, including both scarp and plateau. The word cliff occurs in both Old English (*clif*) and Old Norse (*klif*).

ABOVE: **Lincoln Edge from Harmston Low Fields, Kesteven**

RIGHT: **Lincoln Edge from Broxholme, Lindsey**

Lincoln (see next chapter), the scarp is unbroken and forms a continuous natural bulwark along the western margin of the limestone uplands. By national standards the Lincoln Edge is undeniably modest, seldom rising more than 150 ft (46m), yet its striking linearity and wide views in the otherwise flat landscape emphasise its topographic significance. It also forms a local boundary for weather, often dividing upland sun from Vale fog, or vice versa, and creating a temperature differential between snowy upland and unfrozen fields below. There is a gradual decline in the elevation of the escarpment northwards, and north of Scampton its gentler contours lose the pastoral land use seen further south. Some sections have blocks of woodland, while a more substantial area of heathland, now mostly afforested, occurs near Scunthorpe where Coversands have accumulated.

The rock formation creating the Lincoln Edge is called the Inferior Oolite, which includes the famous Lincolnshire Limestone. This provides a hard capping at the top of the scarp, protecting the softer mudstones which form the bulk of the slope below. In places, a sandy ironstone – the Northampton Sand formation – sits directly beneath the Oolite, yielding ore that has been mined historically at Greetwell and Coleby near Lincoln and also on the plateau around Colsterworth. However, it is the limestones which are the dominant player in terms of landscape. Back from the scarp, they form a plateau several miles wide, slowly declining eastwards. For centuries this provided rough grazing on limestone 'heath' until its reclamation and enclosure for farmland in the late 1800s (see Chapter 7).

The Lincoln Edge has been a remarkable organising feature of the human landscape, both as a routeway and in the pattern of villages, parishes and fields. Use of the crest of the escarpment as a 'way' probably started in the Mesolithic, when bands of hunter-gatherers were moving considerable distances across Britain in search for food and to exchange valued goods. Conjecturally, by the Neolithic, it formed part of a more permanent routeway, termed the Jurassic Way, linking ultimately with south-west England (see Chapter 4). Today, sections of this assumed route are still in use as footpaths and roads, including the Viking Way between Wellingore and Lincoln, and Middle Street north of the city. The landscape has obviously been transformed repeatedly over the millennia, yet the exhilaration of wide views, spectacular sunsets and the sense of travelling along a natural causeway with linear intent can still be experienced today.

The origin of settlement along the Lincoln Edge is more speculative. The scarp's spring line and vantage points probably attracted camps as early as the Mesolithic, such as at Willoughton. Later, in the Anglo-Saxon period, settlement 'nucleation' produced the pattern of Medieval 'cliff villages' that essentially survives today. These range in position between the top and base of the scarp, but the settlement line runs continuously from Croxton Kerrial (Leics) to Winteringham overlooking the Humber. Each villlage has a share of the limestone plateau and, except where the ironstone intervenes, of clay vale land, known south of Lincoln as Low Fields. This has produced a strongly axial pattern with elongated parishes at right angles to the Lincoln Edge. Parish boundaries are often marked by hedgelines that sweep down the scarp and into the Vale of Trent for a distance of a mile or

FACING PAGE: **Lincoln Edge viewpoint, South Carlton**

22

more. Later field boundaries reflect the same axis. Thus, developments in farming over centuries have reinforced or repeated the same axial geometry based on underlying geology and the need to access a range of resources.

More than any other escarpment in Lincolnshire, the Lincoln Edge has attracted country houses, providing their occupants with a combination of expansive views and a ready-made setting for the latest fashion in landscaping. This is particularly so in Kesteven, where the succession of cliff-top halls south of Lincoln includes Harmston, Coleby, Boothby Graffoe and Wellingore. Further south, Belton House and Harlaxton Manor are on a grander scale and have utilised the Edge in their landscaped parkland.

The Cretaceous escarpments: Lincolnshire Wolds

Several miles east of the Jurassic Oolites, beyond the clay-based flatlands of the Lindsey Vale and Fens, the next and final escarpment belongs to the Cretaceous rocks. This lies within Lincolnshire only in the northern half of the county where, in Lindsey, it announces the start of the Lincolnshire Wolds. South of here, the Wash intervenes and the Cretaceous escarpment disappears until Norfolk is reached, rising again as a more subdued feature sometimes called the Norfolk Edge.

FACING PAGE: **Caistor Wolds from Nettleton Beck**

TOP RIGHT: **Sixhills church on the Wolds escarpment**

RIGHT: **Wolds escarpment north of Walesby**

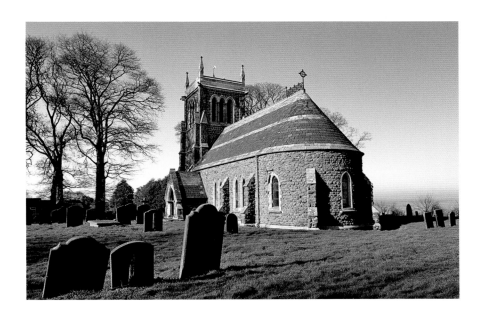

25

Chalk grassland would once have been common in the chalk areas of the Lincolnshire Wolds, especially on the chalk escarpments, supporting a calcareous grassland . However, most of this has been either ploughed or improved as part of the agricultural changes that occured from Parliamentary enclosure onwards. Today, chalk grassland is rare in the Wolds, being restricted to a few locations on the escarpment that are too steep to plough and some old quarry margins, now mostly managed as local nature reserves. Additionally, roadside verges can support limestone flora if managed sensitively, as surveyed and promoted by Lincolnshire Wildlife Trust and its partners through the 'Life on the Verge' initiative (see www.lincstrust.org.uk).

LEFT: **chalk scarp at Rowgate Hill, Wolds**

BOTTOM LEFT: **Autumn gentian (*Gentianella amarella*) in bloom, Red Hill, Wolds**

If the Lincoln Edge fuses geology and historic patterns of land use in an ordered, almost geometric landscape influenced strongly by genteel aesthetics, the Cretaceous scarp is more naturalistic and in places has an altogether wilder quality. It encompasses Lincolnshire's highest land and boldest terrain, with the section between Nettleton and Walesby being particularly notable for its dramatic landscape. Normanby Top is the highest point in the county at 550 ft (168m) and has views stretching to the Trent Valley, Pennines and Yorkshire Wolds. Looked at more closely, the Cretaceous escarpment is really two scarps, sometimes conjoined and at other times diverging. The 'active' ingredients are, firstly, the sandstones, ironstones and limestones of the Lower Cretaceous – including the Spilsby Sandstone and Tealby Limestone – and, secondly, the overlying Chalk formation. Near the Humber, the Lower Cretaceous is thin and plays only a minor role in the escarpment. Here, between South Ferriby and Elsham, the scarp slope is composed of chalk, presenting pleasant scenery with a mixture of pasture, arable and woodland, with occasional chalk quarries. A line of Medieval villages runs along the foot of the scarp, each elongated parish having its share of upland pasture on the Wolds and former carr land in the Ancholme valley. A similar pattern continues south of the Barnetby Gap to Caistor, though here the villages are set back from the wetlands and have lowlands based on sands and gravels.

The central, high section of the escarpment between Caistor and Sixhills is a composite feature of Lower Cretaceous strata capped by chalk. This section is defined by steeply incised valleys, rough slopes with damp, rushy pasture and the remains of former ironstone mining (Squires, 2017). South of Sixhills, the scarp splits in two, with the twin elements first running in parallel to Belchford, then parting completely. The Lower Cretaceous scarp loses its steepness and definition here, becoming more of an upslope to a ridge of land that pushes slowly south-east past Horncastle to Spilsby. Conversely, the chalk escarpment becomes bolder, trending south-east to Candlesby. It mostly lacks the upland quality seen further north, but has steep slopes with woodland and pasture. This is the closest Lincolnshire comes to the chalk downs of southern England.

Patterns of human interaction along the southern portion of the Wolds scarp are generally more diffuse than north of Sixhills. Medieval village

27

settlement lacks the strongly axial parishes seen along the northern scarp. Nevertheless, the chalk escarpment and adjoining plateau were an important resource, providing grazing, warrening, lime and building stone for the nearby villages. Clusters of Neolithic and Bronze Age monuments suggest prehistoric occupation occurred throughout the chalk uplands, not just along the escarpment. However, two major prehistoric trackways of the Wolds – High Street and the Bluestone Heath Road – developed close to the escarpments, both surviving in use today as roads (see Chapter 4).

ABOVE: **chalk masonry, Haugh church, Wolds.** Chalk is uncommon as a building stone, but is occasionally seen in older buildings in or near the Wolds. Tealby Limestone and Spilsby Sandstone have been more widely used for building.

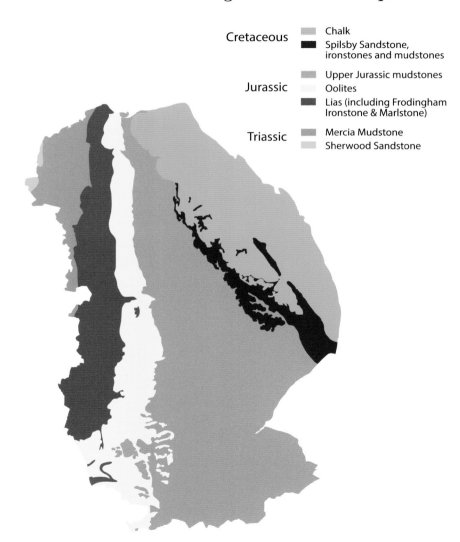

The Main Escarpments in Lincolnshire

Lincolnshire's Bedrock: Age & Main Rock Groups

Cretaceous

Chalk

Spilsby Sandstone, ironstones and mudstones

Upper Jurassic mudstones

Jurassic

Oolites

Lias (including Frodingham Ironstone & Marlstone)

Triassic

Mercia Mudstone

Sherwood Sandstone

Winteringham
Barton-upon-Humber
Burton-upon-Stather
SCUNTHORPE
Barnetby-le-Wold
GRIMSBY
Messingham
Kirton-in-Lindsey
Caistor
Tealby
LOUTH
GAINSBOROUGH
Donington-on-Bain
Belchford
LINCOLN
Horncastle
Candlesby
Bracebridge Heath
SKEGNESS
Leadenham
Caythorpe
SLEAFORD
Ancaster
BOSTON
Belvoir Castle
GRANTHAM
Denton
STAMFORD

— Trent Cliff *(Lower Lias)*

— Marlstone *(Middle Lias)*

— Lincoln Edge *(Oolites)*

— Wolds *(Lower Cretaceous)*

— Wolds *(Chalk)*

0   10   20 km

Contains OS data © Crown copyright and Land-Form Panorama data (2016)

29

References

Fox, J. (2015), *The Lincolnshire Landscape: An Exploration*,
Green Plover Books, Lincoln

Hewlett, H.B. (1935, reprinted 1979), *The Quarries: Ironstone, Limestone and Sand*, Market Overton Industrial Railway Association, Cottesmore, Rutland

Squires, S. (2017), *Ironstone Mining in the Lincolnshire Wolds*, Society for Lincolnshire History & Archaeology

Swinnerton, H.H. & Kent, P.E. (1976), *The Geology of Lincolnshire*, Lincolnshire Naturalists' Union

Tonks, E. (1991), *The Ironstone Quarries of the Midlands: History, Operation & Railways – Part VIII South Lincolnshire*, Runpast Publishing

ABOVE: **Wolds escarpment north of Walesby**

2 : TRENT VALLEYS
Changing Courses, Gaps & the Ice Age

Rivers are one of the most significant linear features in the landscape, both physically and culturally, forming corridors with their own natural processes and ecology that have interracted with human societies from the earliest times. Archaeological remains from over half a million years ago indicate that early hominids used the main river valleys of south-eastern Britain to navigate and colonise the interior of what was then a peninsula of Europe. The 'Bytham River', which crossed southern Lincolnshire prior to the Anglian glaciation, is an important example. Later, despite the risk of flooding, rivers attracted permanent settlement at key crossing and trading points, some of which developed over time into our most important towns. This chapter focuses on the River Trent – including its previous courses through Ancaster and Lincoln – and investigates how the river's evolution during the Ice Age has influenced the landscape across Lincolnshire.

The River Trent is sometimes seen as rather peripheral to Lincolnshire or, at most, as boundary territory with neighbouring counties. However, excepting the estuarial River Humber, the Trent is easily the largest river draining territory in Lincolnshire today. As explained later, it also has

previous courses dating to the Ice Age that affected much of southern and central Lincolnshire. At various points in the Trent's history, its tributaries have included the Witham, Till, Slea, Glen and Bain, and even the Welland and Nene probably joined it before entering the North Sea until relatively recently (Bridgland, 2014). Today's Trent, conjoined with the Ouse to form the Humber, receives the River Ancholme and also affects patterns of silt deposition on Lincolnshire's coast. In short, very little of Lincolnshire is without some Trent influence on its landscape.

FACING PAGE: **River Trent from Trent Cliff at sunset**

RIGHT: **Lincoln Gap at dawn.** The River Trent flowed through the Lincoln Gap for at least 200,000 years up to the end of the Ice Age.

Central to an understanding of the Trent's evolution is the Ice Age or Pleistocene and its cycle of cold and warm stages, termed 'glacials' and 'interglacials'. During cold stages, ice sheets advanced into Britain, sometimes though not invariably reaching as far south as Lincolnshire. It is generally accepted that the major changes in the course of the Trent occurred during or shortly after such glaciations, and were caused directly or indirectly by ice sheets. By contrast, during the interglacials and in cold but unglaciated conditions, the river episodically laid down deposits of sand and gravel called 'terraces', with more localised changes of course sometimes occurring. The maps on page 44 show the main courses of the Trent with reference to Lincolnshire over the last half million years.

The main evidence for former courses lies in the location and composition of the surviving terrace deposits. Rock fragments or 'clasts' within the gravels indicate the river's catchment area and age, as can any fossil remains or human artefacts. As north-west Europe has risen overall during the last

The impacts of glaciation in Lincolnshire are less obvious than in the mountainous parts of Britain, but have nevertheless moulded much of the natural landscape. As well as rerouting major rivers, two key glacial processes were erosion by ice and meltwaters and the deposition of material carried by ice. Ponding back of glacial meltwater seasonally and in warming periods led to overflow channels being carved in the uplands. Numerous examples can be seen cutting across watersheds between valleys in the Wolds, as here near **Swaby** (TOP LEFT). Glacial till deposits remain over large areas of Lincolnshire's surface, as exposed here at **South Ferriby** (LEFT), while the low ridge of land jutting into the Fens at Stickney and Sibsey originated as a 'terminal moraine' of material at the western limit of the Devensian ice sheets.

million years, river terraces occupy successively higher levels in the landscape with age, further assisting their dating and correlation.

The Ancaster Trent: tributary of the ancient Bytham River and route for early humans?

The origin of the River Trent in geological time remains largely a matter of conjecture, though it seems likely that a precursor of the river existed from early in the Quaternary period and possibly even earlier. The first sedimentary evidence for the Trent so far identified is river gravel near Ancaster, dating to the late Cromerian or early Anglian prior to glaciation. Since the 1930s, geologists have postulated that an ancestral Trent flowed via Ancaster, but this has only recently been confirmed. A spread of gravel at North Rauceby – the Rauceby Gravel – is now interpreted as a terrace of the main river, with a tributary stream depositing the nearby Caythorpe Heath Gravel. These deposits are thought to be the oldest Trent gravels surviving anywhere in the river's catchment today (Bridgland, 2014).

The position of these ancient river deposits on top of the Jurassic limestone plateau indicates that the present Ancaster Gap was incised later as the land

TOP RIGHT: **near North Rauceby.** The area west of North Rauceby village is the location of the Rauceby Gravel, the oldest known Trent deposit surviving today.

RIGHT: **the Ancaster Gap near Wilsford**

rose. It is likely that the Ancaster Trent started to cut into the limestone, but that incision of the current Gap was undertaken by the River Slea after the Trent had shifted north following the Anglian glaciation. At this time, the upper Witham was probably an upstream continuation of the Slea, as evidenced by surviving gravel spreads which occupy the floor of the Gap and also extend south-west towards Grantham.

Relatively little is certain about the Ancaster Trent, but it was probably smaller and shorter than its successors. The current Trent catchment above Nottingham at that time drained into a much larger river system to the south, known as the Bytham River. During the Cromerian, the latter flowed from near Stratford-upon-Avon (Warwicks) to a North Sea coastline close to that of East Anglia today, cutting a major river gap through the Jurassic Oolites in south Lincolnshire between South Witham and Castle Bytham. The 'Bytham Gap' was completely infilled with glacial deposits during the Anglian glaciation, but its buried form survives in the limestone bedrock. Based on comparison of gravel deposits and river gradients, many geologists think the Ancaster Trent is likely to have been a tributary of

LEFT: **Rauceby Warren, Ancaster Gap.** Rauceby Warren is an area of grassy heathland based on riverine sand and gravel known as the Belton Gravel. This deposit occupies the floor of the Ancaster Gap and also extends up the Witham valley through Barkston to Belton near Grantham. The Belton Gravel is thought to post-date the Ancaster Trent and was probably laid down by the River Slea in the middle of the Ice Age, at which time this river also drained the upper Witham catchment. Tentatively, the river catchment above Barkston was then 'captured' by the middle Witham as a tributary of the Lincoln Trent, leaving the Ancaster Gap as the dry coll that exists today.

LEFT: **Castle Bytham.** The picturesque stone village of Castle Bytham lies on a small stream in the quiet countryside of the Kesteven Uplands near Bourne. Half a million years ago, one of Britain's largest rivers of the time, the Bytham River, cut through the Jurassic Oolites here in a valley that is thought to have been an important migration route for early humans. The earliest known human artefacts in Britain have recently been discovered at East Anglian sites close to former estuaries of the Bytham River at Pakefield (Suffolk) and Happisburgh (Norfolk), dating to 700,000 and 850,000 or 950,000 years ago respectively (Dinnis & Stringer, 2013). It is therefore possible that human presence in Lincolnshire also goes back to this time, much earlier than previously thought.

the Bytham River, and probably joined the latter in what is now the Fens en route to East Anglia (Bridgland, 2014).

In addition to their geological interest, the Bytham River deposits have yielded important archaeological finds of early Palaeolithic age in East Anglia and the Midlands, including early stone tools, though sadly not within Lincolnshire so far. Nevertheless, these finds strongly suggest early human presence in south Lincolnshire, with use of the Bytham valley here as a

regional route for migration and colonisation, potentially also encompassing tributary valleys such as the Ancaster Trent.

The climate at the time of the Ancaster Trent and Bytham River was temperate initially, becoming boreal as conditions cooled towards the Anglian glaciation. The latter saw complete human abandonment of the British peninsula as the ice sheets advanced, and a drastic remoulding of Lincolnshire's topography and drainage. Between roughly 450,000 and

425,000 years ago Britain was severely glaciated, and many established landscape features were transformed by ice sheets and their meltwaters. At this time, ice is thought to have instigated the Wash 'gap' in the chalk bridge between Lincolnshire and Norfolk, and also excavated the Fen Basin. The Bytham River vanished due to plugging of its gap and obliteration of the lower course across the Fen basin.

As deglaciation ensued, the Trent appears to have abandoned Ancaster in favour of a more northerly course, most probably through the Lincoln Gap to the newly formed Wash. The reason for this shift is uncertain, but may have been the availability of a new channel carved by glacial meltwaters and/or uneven rebounding of land behind the retreating ice sheets.

36

The Lincoln Trent: an extinct valley through Lincoln to the Wash

It has long been known that the River Trent flowed through the Lincoln Gap at some point in the Ice Age, based on gravels found nearby in the Witham valley. Until recently, it was widely believed that this was due to the Trent's diversion during one or more glacial episodes when ice blocked the Humber. However, new evidence has shown that the Trent flowed through Lincoln to the Wash for a much longer period, following a course that was established with certainty after the Wragby glaciation around 240,000 years ago, and probably much earlier from the end of the Anglian glaciation. The present course to the Humber emerged only after the final glaciation of the Ice Age around 17,000 years ago (Bridgland, 2014).

As there are no known river deposits surviving for the lower Trent between the Anglian and Wragby glaciations, a course via Lincoln at this time is speculative, it being equally possible that it flowed to the Humber in a now vanished valley. However, firm sedimentary evidence for the Lincoln course begins with the Wragby glaciation, after which the Trent laid down a series of gravel terraces that can still be traced from Newark-on-Trent to Lincoln and also downstream of Lincoln along what is now the Witham valley (see map on page 38). These terraces record successive local movements in the river's route over a period of some

LEFT: **Brayford Pool, Lincoln**

FACING PAGE: **mist along the former Trent valley from Lincoln Castle**

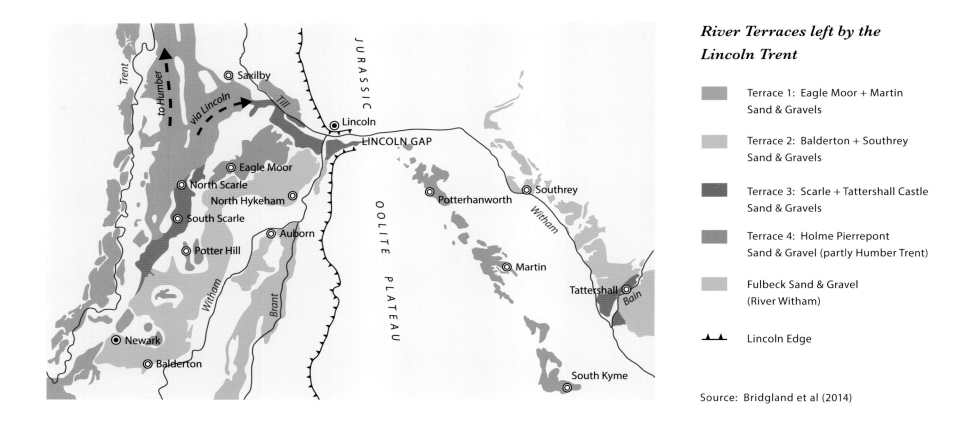

River Terraces left by the Lincoln Trent

- **Terrace 1:** Eagle Moor + Martin Sand & Gravels
- **Terrace 2:** Balderton + Southrey Sand & Gravels
- **Terrace 3:** Scarle + Tattershall Castle Sand & Gravels
- **Terrace 4:** Holme Pierrepont Sand & Gravel (partly Humber Trent)
- Fulbeck Sand & Gravel (River Witham)
- Lincoln Edge

Source: Bridgland et al (2014)

38

220,000 years and, as explained later, have yielded nationally important information about the climate and ecology of this period of the Ice Age.

Looking first at the extinct course from Newark to Lincoln, this still defines the landscape here. The relatively poor gravel soils are manifested as former 'moors', now mostly wooded, while commercial extraction of gravel has created a string of flooded pits with value for wildlife and recreation.

Curiously, Terrace 1, the oldest in the sequence, now occupies hilltop locations, having been uplifted as the land rose and acted as a protective cap for the soft Liassic clays. Sometimes known within Lincolnshire as the Graffoe Hills, this gently elevated land includes Danethorpe Hill (Notts), Brills Hill, Potter Hill, Hill Holt Wood, Eagle Moor and Doddington. Incised between the Graffoe Hills is Terrace 2, the Balderton Sand & Gravel, the best-preserved and arguably most interesting of the Lincoln Trent deposits. Commencing around 240,000 years ago, its deposition spans a complete warm to cold climate cycle after the Wragby glaciation, as dated by faunal and floral remains. These include an impressive array of mammalian bones – mammoth, woolly rhinoceros, bison, lion, wolf, reindeer and brown bear – now housed in the National Museum of Scotland. The absence of hippopotamus suggests that the river had abandoned Terrace 2 before the warm Ipswichian Interglacial. Sadly, no Ipswichian deposits survive for the Lincoln Trent itself, but the Fulbeck Sand & Gravel was probably laid down at this time by its tributary, the River Witham, along what is now the Brant valley and has yielded hippopotamus. The third and fourth terraces record the Lincoln Trent's move north-west through the Scarles and Saxilby and its ultimate shift north to the Humber, covering the Devensian stages of the Ice Age.

Downstream of the Lincoln Gap, each of the Lincoln Trent terraces has a correlate along what is now the Witham valley. Here too, the older terraces occupy higher ground, capping the gentle hills that fringe the wide alluvial valley as far as South Kyme and Tattershall. These produce a landscape of infertile former 'moors' similar to that noted above. As this section of valley was taken over by the orphaned River Witham when it was abandoned by

Sand and gravel deposited by the Lincoln Trent still exerts a major landscape influence between Newark and Lincoln. These two scenes are of former gravel workings in the Balderton Sand & Gravel at **Swanholme Lakes, Lincoln** (TOP RIGHT) and **near Thurlby** (RIGHT).

FACING PAGE: **the Witham valley from Metheringham Barff.**
The broad valley of the Witham below Lincoln was the route of the
Lincoln Trent for up to 400,000 years before the Trent shifted course
to the Humber at the end of the Ice Age. Trent gravels from the
period before the move occupy the valley floor but are covered by
later silts, partly of marine origin. The older Trent terraces occupy
the higher valley sides due to uplift and valley incision, as here at
Metheringham Barff, which is capped by the Martin Sand & Gravel.

RIGHT: **heathland, Kirkby Moor.** Sands and gravels washed
down from the Wolds were deposited extensively in the Woodhall
Spa area by the River Bain towards the end of the Devensian
glaciation, forming outwash spreads in Lake Fenland. The latter
developed when glacial ice blocked the Wash, trapping the Lincoln
Trent and other Fenland rivers and glacial meltwaters. Today, Kirkby
Moor is the largest surviving area of heathland in Lincolnshire and
is managed as a nature reserve due to its high ecological value.

41

the Trent, it continued to evolve as an 'active' valley even after the Ice
Age. The valley also connects to the Fen basin and experienced the changes
in sea level and marine incursions affecting the wider basin and the Wash
(see Chapter 3). Consequently, the youngest deposits of the Lincoln Trent
are covered here by later silts of mainly tidal origin. Nevertheless, the Lincoln
Trent continued to have a significant landscape influence until the very
end. In the Devensian glaciation, the river was blocked by ice in the Wash
and ponded back, contributing to Lake Fenland. Outwash spreads of sand
and gravel were deposited on the lake's edge by the River Bain and now
support extensive heathland around Woodhall Spa.

Relatively little is known about human interaction with the Lincoln Trent.
Neanderthals were apparently present when deposition of Terrace 2 began,
based on finds of stone tools in the area, but they are thought to have
vanished due to cold conditions around 180,000 years ago. Hominids were
then absent from Britain for some 100,000 years. Neanderthals recolonised
the region, followed by modern humans, while the later Trent terraces
were being laid down, during 'mammoth steppe' conditions prior to and
following the Devensian glaciation. Stone handaxes of the period preceding
this glaciation have been found in Lincolnshire at Fillingham, Harlaxton
and Risby Warren (Bridgland, 2014).

The Lincoln Gap itself is a remarkable focal point in Lincolnshire's landscape that almost certainly held human significance before the oldest (Mesolithic) archaeological finds in the area. Its origins are unclear, however, due mainly to the lack of older river sediments here. Geologists have postulated a gap dating back to the Tertiary period, but this is highly speculative. Nevertheless, it is possible that the Lincoln Trent usurped the valley gap of an earlier 'Lincoln River' following the Anglian glaciation. Alternatively, the gap may have been primarily glacio-fluvial in origin, perhaps carved by the overflow from a glacial lake. Successive glacial and river events may have reinforced the gap following an initial breach in the limestone. In any case, the Lincoln Trent almost certainly enlarged the gap considerably, given the river's longevity here and its status today as England's second largest river by volume of water. The broad, abandoned gap of the Trent has thus provided the setting for Lincoln's urban development over the past two millennia and still defines the city's shape today.

The Humber Trent: a new course for modern times

The Trent's move to the Humber occurred around 17,000 years ago as the Devensian glaciers retreated. The most likely cause is the creation of a new channel by meltwaters overflowing south from glacial Lake Humber. The Humber Trent is therefore different from its Ice Age predecessors in having witnessed the accelerating landscape changes wrought by humans from the Mesolithic to the present. Initially, the Humber Trent may have acted as a barrier for people, as valley and estuarial wetlands developed. However, the river also became a major route from early in its history, facilitating

The present Trent Valley in Lincolnshire encompasses the river's change
in character from middle age to the more obviously tidal lower reaches
below Gainsborough. From Dunham Bridge, the river snakes through
its alluvial floodplain between low bluffs of Triassic Mercia Mudstone. In
places the latter form more substantial features, including Newton Cliff,
Red Hill near Knaith (FACING PAGE), the Gainsborough escarpment and
Hardwick Hill in Laughton Forest. The bluffs and valley bottom together
form a distinct trench in the Mercia Mudstone, possibly representing the
eoded remains of the conjectural glacial overflow channel that provided
the Trent with its new route northwards after the Devensian glaciation.
The lower Trent is at its most industrial around Gunness Bridge and
Flixborough, then unexpectedly passes the escarpment of **Trent Cliff**
(RIGHT) before joining with Yorkshire's Ouse to form the River Humber.

BOTTOM RIGHT: **River Trent near Susworth**

43

movement, settlement, trade and even invasion. In AD 872 - 3, the Danish
army established a camp at Torksey before pushing into Mercia the
following year, while King Sweyn Forkbeard, father of King Canute,
led his successful invasion force via the Trent in 1013. Throughout
history the Trent has therefore been something of a paradox, forming
a natural boundary whilst also providing connectivity to the outside
world. Today, the distances between bridges tends to emphasise
the river as an obstacle, and it should be noted that numerous ferry
crossings existed historically, some into the 20th century. The river's
trade was also far greater in the past, with Gainsborough developing
into one of England's largest inland ports by the late 18th century.

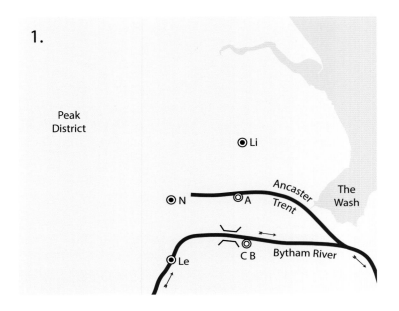

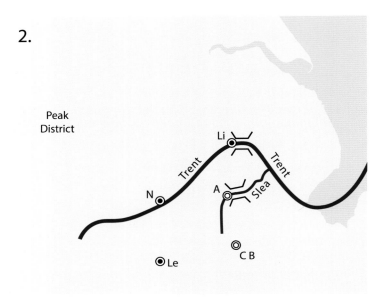

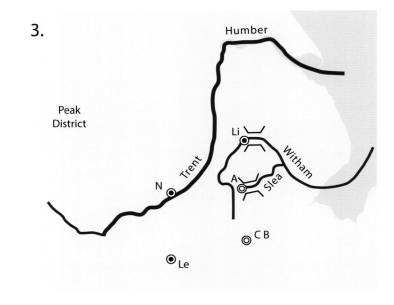

Former courses of the River Trent:

- *Map 1 : Ancaster Trent and Bytham River*
  before the Anglian glaciation (c. 600,000 years ago)

- *Map 2 : Lincoln Trent after the Wragby glaciation*
  (c. 240,000 years ago)

- *Map 3 : Humber Trent after the Devensian glaciation*
  (c. 17,000 years ago)

A = Ancaster; CB = Castle Bytham; Le = Leicester; Li = Lincoln; N = Nottingham

Source: Bridgland et al (2014)

References

Bridgland, D. et al (eds) (2014), *Quaternary of the Trent*, Oxbow Books

Buckland, P.C., *North-West Lincolnshire 10,0000 Years Ago*, in Field, N. and White, A. (1984), *A Prospect of Lincolnshire*, Field & White, Lincoln

Knight, D. & Howard, A.J. (2004), *Trent Valley Landscapes*, Heritage Marketing and Publications Ltd

Straw, A. (2002), *Lincolnshire - gaps and more gaps*, in Geology Today, Volume 18, No. 1, January - February 2002

Straw, A. (2008), *The Last Two Glaciations of East Lincolnshire*, Louth Naturalists', Antiquarian and Literary Society & Lincolnshire Naturalists' Union

RIGHT: **Coversands heath at Spalford Warren (Notts), Trent Valley.** Wind-blown sands or Coversands are the final legacy of the Devensian in Lincolnshire. These survive widely in the north-west of the county, and are thought to have been spread across the landscape by westerly winds in tundra conditions following de-glaciation. The source of the material was probably sand left by glaciers, lakes and rivers, especially the Trent, originally derived mainly from Triassic sandstones further west. Today, Coversands support heathland on mainly acidic soils, though large areas have been lost to afforestation, mineral extraction, farming and urban development.

3 : COASTLINES
Past & Present Edges of the Land

The coastline is perhaps the most fundamental linear feature that occurs in the natural landscape – the place where land meets sea. The width and character of coastlines varies with local geology and topography, being abrupt and relatively narrow in the case of sea cliffs but often much broader in a predominantly low-lying and level context such as Lincolnshire's coast. Some therefore prefer to describe the latter as a zone rather than a line, as tidal environments and marine influence can extend for several miles inland via creeks and rivers. This was particularly so before sea banks and sluices artificially defined the high tide line, and should be borne in mind when considering past coastlines in Lincolnshire.

Coastlines have been important for humans in Britain from the outset. The earliest human inhabitants of what was then the British peninsula probably arrived along the coastline from continental Europe around 900,000 years ago, leaving flint artefacts and footprints in East Anglia. While some colonists struck inland via the main river valleys, other communities focused on the coast to exploit the varied resources the latter provided. In essence, this picture has been repeated with each human recolonisation of Britain through the Ice Age and again in the early Mesolithic. Later, during the Anglo-Saxon period, coastal communities in Lincolnshire established the lines of primary settlements which still exist around the Wash and in the Lindsey Marsh, from which Medieval expansion and land reclamation occurred. A millennium later, much of the Lincolnshire coast is characterised by holiday resorts, caravan parks and port developments, yet still retains stretches of wilder coastline that include some of Europe's most important wildlife habitats.

47

FACING PAGE: **relict cliff of 125,000 years ago, North Thoresby, Wolds**

RIGHT: **present coastline, Saltfleetby-Theddlethorpe**

48

While these historical developments define the character of the modern coastline, it is the longer-term pattern of shifts in the position of the coast that has perhaps been its most significant landscape contribution. This chapter looks at Lincolnshire's coastal evolution since the beginning of the Ice Age, focusing particularly on previous coastlines which have a physical manifestation as linear features in the landscape today. The map on page 60 illustrates the main such coastlines through history.

All change: Lincolnshire's shifting coastline

Regular visitors to the Lincolnshire coast have probably observed changes in its natural geography over a period of just a few years, as features such as dunes, beaches and saltmarsh can appear, move or vanish well within a human lifetime. In more sheltered sections of the coastline with a supply of marine silt and sand, as at Gibraltar Point and Donna Nook, outward growth has occurred naturally over several centuries, resulting in a complex succession of new 'coastlines', each typically marked by a new spit or dune system. Land reclamation using sea banks and/or saltern waste has exploited this natural coastal aggradation since Anglo-Saxon times. By contrast, the more exposed stretch of coastline between Skegness and Mablethorpe has long experienced erosion. Today, the balance may be

LEFT: **North Sea, Theddlethorpe St. Helen**

FACING PAGE: **old dune line, North Cotes**

shifting towards erosion, but Lincolnshire's coast was already a dynamic zone well before man-made global warming was added to the mix.

Taking a longer timescale, much greater changes in the position of the coast have occurred, mainly as a result of fluctuations in land and sea level related to the glacial cycle of the Ice Age. Broadly, warm interglacial conditions with higher relative sea level pushed the coastal zone further inland than at present, sometimes even reaching the margins of the Wolds and Jurassic uplands. Modelling of the Lincoln Trent (see Chapter 2) indicates that around 300,000 years ago, estuarial conditions extended right through the Lincoln Gap as far upstream as the Newark area, with a tidal River Trent flowing here, akin to the present Humber. Conversely, periods with lower sea levels than at present, during and either side of glaciations, saw the coastline positioned further east and north and, at times, nowhere near the area we now call Lincolnshire. As recently as 8,500 years ago during the early Mesolithic period, a continuous land bridge existed between Lincolnshire and what is now the Netherlands.

FACING PAGE: the landscape of the Wash c. 500,000 years ago? This chalkland scene in the **LIncolnshire Wolds** is how the Wash area might have looked before the chalk ridge between Lincolnshire and Norfolk was breached in the Anglian glaciation. In interglacial stages, woodland may have colonised the now vanished chalk hills, but steppe grassland or tundra would have prevailed when climatic conditions were colder. It is not known whether humans ever traversed these hills but it is a strong possibility. At this time, the Wolds would also have been higher and extended further east than now. The ice sheets of the Anglian glaciation subsequently initiated the development of the Wash by erosion of the chalk ridge.

Beginnings: the coastline of Lincolnshire's first humans

As seen in Chapter 1, an identifiable precursor landscape of modern Lincolnshire had probably emerged by the start of the Quaternary or perhaps some time before, with the upland belts of the Oolites and Wolds and a North Sea coastline somewhere to the east, the latter moving its position in response to the glacial cycle. The character of this early Quaternary coastline is uncertain in the absence of geological deposits, but conceivably ranged between saltmarsh and chalk cliffs depending on sea level, as seen later on in the period. However, many geologists think that the Wash did not exist before the Anglian glaciation and that a ridge of chalk hills akin to the present Wolds still connected Lincolnshire and Norfolk. Theoretically, it would therefore have been possible for the early humans of the Cromerian to have walked on dry land between Spilsby and Hunstanton. However, thick forest and/or river gaps may have discouraged movement here and effectively channelled these first hunter-gatherers along the coast or inland along the river valleys.

What is known is that humans were already present on the eastern shore of the British peninsula by either 950,000 or 840,000 years ago, based on archaeological finds discovered recently at Happisburgh on the Norfolk coast (*Dinnis & Stringer, 2013). These artefacts are from an environment which then adjoined a large estuary near the confluence of the pre-Anglian Thames and Bytham Rivers, slightly inland of the coast of the time. They include flint tools that are the oldest known human artefacts in northern Europe, as well the earliest known human footprints outside Africa, probably of the species *Homo antecessor*. Tentatively, it is therefore likely that the first humans to inhabit eastern Britain arrived coastally along an embayment on the north side of the land bridge which joined south-east England to continental Europe. Sadly, unlike in Norfolk and Suffolk, nothing survives of the Cromerian coastal landscape of Lincolnshire in terms of its archaeology or geology – the subsequent Anglian ice sheets apparently obliterated all here. Nevertheless, it is not unreasonable to assume that humans had visited if not actually occupied Lincolnshire's coast before the end of the Cromerian, based on their known presence in East Anglia as well as inland along the Bytham River in the East Midlands (see Chapter 2).

The Anglian glaciation of c. 450-425,000 years ago saw the complete abandonment of Britain and northern Europe by humans, while ice sheets profoundly altered the landscape and drainage of the Lincolnshire area. Recolonisation by early Neanderthal humans occurred after the Anglian glaciation but, unlike in southern England, is thinly evidenced archaeologically in Lincolnshire, so relatively little is known about their communities or living environments here at this time.

The Lincolnshire coast between the Anglian and Wragby glaciations is, like the wider landscape, also largely a matter of speculation. The emergence early in this period of the Wash Gap and, probably, the Trent's diversion via Lincoln to the Wash, strongly suggest the Fen Basin had developed as a new and important element in Lincolnshire's coastal landscape that would have experienced marine incursions and retreats as part of the glacial cycle. As noted above, estuarial conditions probably extended right through the Lincoln Gap during the Purfleet Interglacial of 300,000 years ago.

White cliffs of Lincolnshire: the Ipswichian Interglacial

The Wragby glaciation (c. 275-250,000 years ago) marks the start of a period of sedimentary survival in Lincolnshire, from which its palaeo-geography, ecology and human activity can be reconstructed with greater confidence. However, the first relict coastline observable in Lincolnshire today dates to the subsequent Ipswichian Interglacial centred 125,000 years ago – one of the warmest interglacial stages in the Ice Age. Conditions slightly warmer than those of today allowed species such as hippopotamus to live in Lincolnshire's rivers, while rising sea levels are thought to have flooded the Fen basin and created cliffs along the eastern and southern flanks of the Wolds. Remarkably, this cliffed coastline can still be traced in the landscape, albeit heavily smoothed by the subsequent Devensian ice sheets and partially hidden by the tills they left.

On the eastern edge of the Wolds from the Humber south to Candlesby, the cliffs of chalk were up to 300 ft high and survive today in eroded form as the scarplike feature overlooking the Lindsey Marsh. The existence of a wave-cut platform of chalk beneath the present Marshland suggests that they existed for many millennia, gradually moving west as the sea cut into the Wolds. Further sea cliffs occurred in the Spilsby Sandstone at the southern tip of the Wolds, represented today by the hills rising steeply from the Fens at Kirkby and the Keals. It is possible, though not certain, that sea cliffs also extended around the Fen basin at this time, along the margins of Lincolnshire's Jurassic uplands and the chalk of the East Anglian Heights. Curiously, humans do not appear to have been present in Britain during the Ipswichian. As noted in Chapter 2, evidence indicates that Neanderthals

Some of the highest sea levels experienced by Lincolnshire during the last million years occurred around 125,000 years ago in the Ipswichian Interglacial, which saw the coastline pushed far inland. Towering chalk cliffs developed along the eastern side of the Lincolnshire Wolds, resembling the present-day cliffs at Bempton in Yorkshire. Further sea cliffs extended around the southern flank of the Wolds. Today, the Ipswichian coastline can still be traced in the landscape.

ABOVE: **Hall Hill and the Fens from Hareby**. Hall Hill and the nearby Keal hills rise steeply from the Fens and are thought to represent the eroded remains of Ipswichian sea cliffs of Spilsby Sandstone. In this scene, the modern Wash is just visible as a thin, pale line with the low chalk hills of Norfolk forming the far horizon.

RIGHT: **West Keal church**

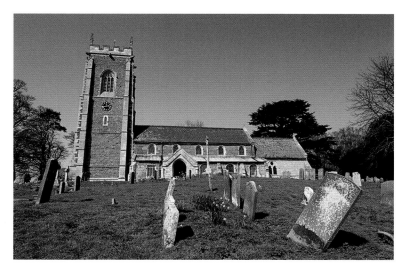

recolonised Britain after the Wragby glaciation but disappeared again in the following cold stage around 180,000 years ago. This abandonment was initially similar to previous ones – a direct response to extreme cold – but was reinforced and prolonged by the creation (or substantial widening) of a proto Dover Strait and massive new Channel River in a catastrophic glacial overflow event. This created a formidable barrier both to humans and wildlife, especially during interglacials when rising seas cut Britain off as an island. Additionally, the interglacial forests of Britain and western Europe at this time may have been unattractive to Neanderthals, whose culture had become increasingly adapted to hunting in cooler, more open environments with migratory megafauna – the 'mammoth steppe'. In Britain, this occurred only transitionally between Arctic and Atlantic phases. In any case, it was at least 100,000 years before humans returned (*Dinnis & Stringer, 2013).

Doggerland to Fenland: submerged forests & 'bog oaks'

Humans may not have witnessed Lincolnshire's version of the white cliffs of Dover while the sea lapped at their base, but the subsequent marine retreat is thought to have left the former cliffline as a major feature in the landscape in the cooling period before the Devensian ice sheets advanced. As sea level dropped again, a land bridge to the Continent was re-established around 70,000 years ago in the North Sea basin. Known as Doggerland,

LEFT: **heathland, Kirkby Moor.** This is how the Wash landscape might have looked when it was still part of Doggerland in the boreal conditions of the early Mesolithic.

this was permanently inhabitated and facilitated recolonisation of the area that is now Britain by late Neanderthals and then by modern humans. However, climatic instability and the limited archaeological record indicates increasingly sporadic and seasonal occupation of Britain from around 45,000 years ago. Speculatively, the former cliffline of the Wolds would at this time have been visible for miles across the Doggerland plains as a long, white scar of chalk that almost certainly held significance for migrating bands of hunter-gatherers, if only as a landmark for navigation.

Yet again it was glaciation that refashioned this landscape. The Devensian glaciation (c. 30-17,000 years ago) saw ice sheets advance west onto the Lincolnshire Wolds, effectively smoothing off and burying the old chalk cliffline and its foreshore. Tills left by these ice sheets still survive extensively in east Lincolnshire, covering the inland portion of the Lindsey Marsh (Middle Marsh) and parts of the Wolds. Ice sheets also blocked the Humber and the Wash, ponding back their rivers into large lakes – Lake Humber and Lake Fenland – and probably instigating the rerouting of the River Trent northwards to the Humber (see Chapter 2).

Climatic amelioration following the retreat of the Devensian glaciers was not smooth. An initial warming stage – the Windermere Interstadial – saw

55

Intertidal expanses and saltmarshes probably typified the retreating coastline of Doggerland as sea levels rose through the Mesolithic period.

TOP RIGHT: **saltmarsh near Rimac**

RIGHT: **sandflats and creek at low tide, Saltfleet**

colonisation of the British peninsula by dwarf willow, mammoth and modern humans of Cresswellian culture, who probably arrived from the east across Doggerland. However, this was interrupted by arctic conditions again from 12,900 to 11,700 years ago – the Loch Lomond Stadial – when humans probably abandoned Lincolnshire for a final time. Their return marks the start of the Mesolithic, as well as our own geological epoch, the Holocene, with its relatively warm if fluctuating climate. From a low point of over 410 ft (125m) below the present sea level in the Devensian glaciation, sea level rose again with the warming trend. Doggerland was progressively flooded until, by 8,000 years ago, Britain was fully an island again. The final separation may have occurred when underwater landslides off Norway generated tsunamis which struck Britain's east coast (Waddington, 2014).

Traces of the lost Doggerland landscape can still be found off the present Lincolnshire coast, where sandbanks, shoals, peat deposits and the remains of drowned forests occur (Robinson, 2001). Intriguingly, there is new evidence suggesting that offshore island fragments of Doggerland may have been inhabited into the Neolithic period. However, inundation of Doggerland would progressively have pushed people westwards as refugees and onto the higher land of the British island, including Lincolnshire.

The post-Devensian marine advance continued over several millennia, reaching a maximum in the Fen basin in the Bronze Age, when tidal creeks extended inland to the Kesteven Fen Edge and up the Witham valley almost to Lincoln. As the water table rose, early forests in the Fen basin were drowned and buried in peat, surviving today as 'bog oaks'. Further north, waterlogging instigated the raised peat mires of the

Humberhead Levels. Curiously, sea levels then stabilised for a millennium until the end of the Roman period. This allowed colonisation of the coastal silts and the expansion of early salt production (Lane & Morris, 2001). However, a further marine incursion followed, burying prehistoric and Roman coastal surfaces under several feet of silt. Recolonisation of these silts then led ultimately to the coastal settlement patterns we see today.

The Medieval coastline: villages, sea banks and salterns

The next coastline to have left a significant physical legacy is that of Medieval times. Commencing in the Anglo-Danish period, much of Lincolnshire's coast underwent consolidation as communities sought to control tidal flooding and reclaim land. This followed on from a process of settlement 'nucleation' which established fixed and focused villages in an arc around the Wash and along the seaward margin of the Middle Marsh. These 'primary' settlements were the focus for reclamation of coastal marshland and the creation of 'daughter' settlements on new coastlines.

Sea banks predominated for reclamation and tidal defence around the Wash, whereas raised land created from saltern waste was probably the initial method of coastal consolidation in parts of the Outmarsh, with banks being added later for protection where required. The coast road between South Somercotes and North Cotes marks the consolidated coast-line here, still referred to as *Seadyke Way* in the 1700s (*Thirsk, 1957).

FACING PAGE: **reclaimed marshland, Saltfleetby St. Clement, Lindsey Marsh**

The Anglo-Danish coastline before expansion can be inferred from the location of the primary settlements, most of which would have been coastal initially. This is arguably the last natural coast in Lincolnshire, as later coastlines were influenced by human efforts in tidal defence and land reclamation. By 1300, a near continuous sea bank had been developed around the Wash (see Chapter 10) and also on stretches of the Lindsey coast where dunes gave insufficient protection (Robinson, 2001).

Lincolnshire's Medieval coastline thrived economically. There were numerous small ports and havens engaged in fishing and trade. Salt, fish and peat were important exports, while Lincolnshire's wool was channelled through the 'staple port' of Boston, then England's greatest wool exporter. Around the Wash, older settlements like Gedney, Holbeach, Spalding, Surfleet and Wrangle were the main havens, while on the Lindsey coast, the Marshland daughter settlements along the reclaimed coast were pre-eminent, including Saltfleethaven and Grainthorpe. The coast's wealth in this period is reflected in fine Medieval churches, above all at Boston.

Coastal reclamation continued to extend Lincolnshire's coastline outwards in places in subsequent centuries: around the Wash; from Saltfleet to North Cotes; and along the Humber Bank. Reclamation of the Wash continued episodically until the 1970s. At North Somercotes, the reclamation of Porter's Marsh and adjoining land in the 1600s created a new coastline at Donna Nook and left former dunes stranded inland.

However, not all of Lincolnshire's Medieval coastline saw expansion. The more exposed stretch between Skegness and Mablethorpe experienced severe erosion in the Tudor period. Several churches were lost to the sea, including the Medieval settlement of Skegness. Stormy conditions in the late 1300s also saw the destruction of a line of sandbanks or islands just off the Medieval coastline here, sand from which created the beaches that still characterise much of Lincolnshire's coastline today.

The present coastline: an uncertain future?

Today's coastline is perhaps best described as an amalgam of the man-made and the natural, reflecting its complex historical development over the last two millennia. Around the Wash and along the Humber, sea banks define the high tide line, while concrete sea defences and 'seabees' augment the coastal dunes between Skegness and Mablethorpe. More dramatic imprints of human activity include the urban and industrial development of Grimsby, Immingham and the coastal resorts. Nevertheless, long stretches of natural shoreline survive, as at Gibraltar Point and Saltfleet, while the Wash is fringed by the largest area of saltmarsh in Europe.

Lincolnshire's coast now faces rising sea levels as it did in the past, but this time augmented by the impacts of man-made climate change. Ultimately, it remains to be seen if the choices and efforts of humanity will prevent the wholesale retreat of the coastline in the present century and beyond.

FACING PAGE: **North Sea at Anderby Creek**

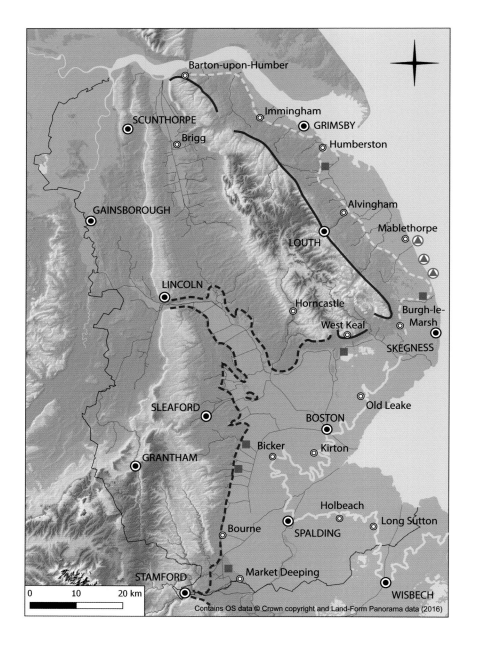

Contains OS data © Crown copyright and Land-Form Panorama data (2016)

Evidence of Former Coastlines in Lincolnshire

IPSWICHIAN INTERGLACIAL (c. 125,000 years ago) - *warm, interglacial conditions saw high sea levels and a coastline of cliffs along the Lincolnshire Wolds. The Fen Basin was under the sea, as probably were the Ancholme and Humberhead lowlands*

—— cliffed coastline along eastern and southern edge of Wolds

- - conjectural coastline around Fen Basin

MESOLITHIC (c. 7,000 years ago) - *the post-glacial rise in sea level had flooded Doggerland and separated off Britain as an island, but the coastline still lay further east than today. Remains of trees from Mesolithic forests survive beneath the low tide line around Huttoft Bank, part of the relict undersea landscape of Doggerland*

⬤ remains of trees and peat off present coastline

BRONZE AGE (c. 4,500 - 2,800 years ago) - *marine incursion reached a peak in the Bronze Age. Forests in the Fen basin were drowned by wetland expansion and the tidal zone reached the Kesteven Fen Edge. Early salterns (saltmaking sites) were located near the high tide line where brine was accessible from tidal creeks*

◼ remains of coastal salterns discovered below present land surface

ANGLO-DANISH (c. 1,100 years ago) - *following deposition of the post-Roman marine silts, resettlement of the Wash coastline occurred. By the AD 800s, nucleated villages were being established on coastal creeks and estuaries here, and on the coastal edge of the Middle Marsh tills in the Lindsey Marsh. Medieval sea banks and reclamation of land commenced in the Anglo-Danish period from c. AD 850 and continued until c. 1300, creating a succession of new, artificial coastlines (see Chapter 10)*

Probable coastline of c. AD 850, based on primary village settlement:

—— coastline of Wash before Medieval sea banks and reclamation

- - edge of tidal zone in Lindsey Marsh before Medieval reclamation

Source: British Geological Survey, MAFF (1983) and Robinson (2001)

References

Ice Age Journeys (www.iceagejourneys.org.uk)

Kime, W. (2005), *The Lincolnshire Seaside*, Sutton Publishing, Stroud

Lane, T. & Morris, E.L. (eds) (2001), *A Millennium of Saltmaking: Prehistoric and Romano-British Salt Production in the Fenland*, Heritage Lincolnshire Report, Heckington

Ministry of Agriculture, Fisheries & Food (1983), *MAFF Map C: The Wash - Green Marsh Areas*, MAFF

Robinson, D.N. (1970), *Coastal Evolution in North-East Lincolnshire* in The East Midland Geographer, Volume 5, Numbers 33 & 34, June - December 1970, University of Nottingham

Robinson, D.N. (2001), *The Book of the Lincolnshire Seaside*, Baron Books, Buckingham

Waddington, C. (2014), *Rescued from the Sea: An Archaeologist's Tale*, Archaeological Research Services & Northumberland Wildlife Trust

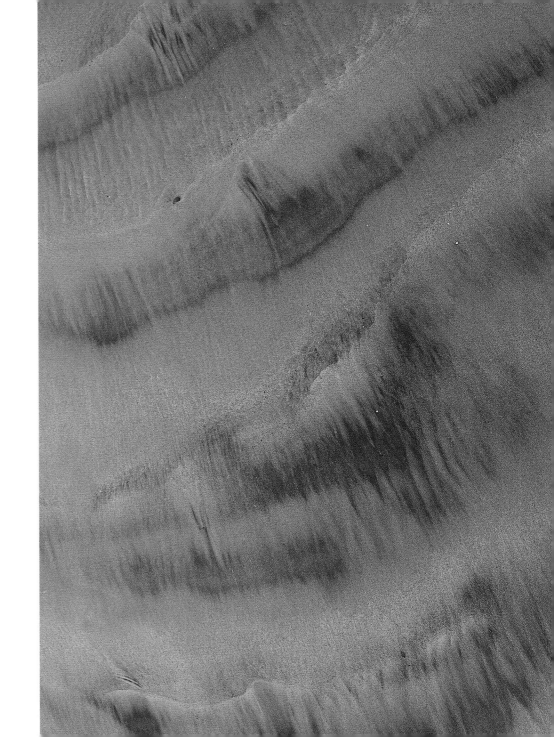

RIGHT: **wave pattern in sand, Theddlethorpe St. Helen**

4 : PREHISTORIC WAYS
Movement of People, Livestock & Salt

We have seen in previous chapters that humans have been crossing the Lincolnshire landscape for at least 800,000 years, often using natural linear features such as valleys, coastlines and escarpments to facilitate travel and navigation. Today, several known or probable routeways from later prehistory survive in Lincolnshire, sometimes still in use as roads, tracks or paths. This chapter explores these ancient routes and their history.

The first pathways: Ice Age hunter-gatherers

The very first human 'ways' in Britain may have developed between glaciations in the Ice Age, now long vanished due to the effects of ice, abandonment and ecological succession. Conjecturally, in periods of human presence, the seasonal movements of hunter-gatherer groups became established as trails used each year, possibly following the migration of prey animals such as reindeer or horse. These may have had some physical or ecological manifestation as 'pathways' through the vegetation, perhaps created by the repeated trampling of herds as seen in the Arctic tundra today. It will probably never be known with certainty if people deliberately

reinforced such routes or made additions such as log bridges or stepping stones across streams or boggy areas. It seems unlikely, though, that sparse populations consisting of small, mobile hunting bands left more than fleeting marks on the natural wilderness of Ice Age Britain.

Following the final glacial retreat and the final (Loch Lomond) cold snap, came the climatic warming of the Mesolithic, commencing some 12,000 years ago. This allowed recolonisation of the British peninsula by modern

63

FACING PAGE: **Ice Age evocation in 2010, Waddington Heath**

RIGHT: **informal path in heathland, Trent Valley**

humans and trees. Initially, pathways were probably transitory as in the Ice Age, being little more than desire lines around temporary camps in the wildwood, maybe utilising tracks created initially by animals like deer and auroch (*Crane, 2016). However, as the population became more settled and the exchange of commodities emerged in the newly created island of Britain, networks of more permanent paths must have developed for travel and trade. Tentatively, by the later Mesolithic, more continuous, long-distance routes emerged to distribute valued items such as the stone axeheads from the Lake District, finds of which occur widely in southern Britain. Evidence for a 'national' ritual culture centred on Neolithic monuments in Wiltshire shows people travelling from all parts of Britain for solstice celebrations, again suggesting established long-distance routes by that time.

In Lincolnshire, the widespread presence of axeheads from other areas of the country clearly implies that transport routes already existed here in the Neolithic, even if materials were arriving by sea or river. Given the human instinct to create and use established pathways with recognisable landmarks and river crossings, it therefore seems likely that 'ways' in Lincolnshire have origins dating back to the Neolithic if not earlier. Moreover, the increasing intensity of farming use and ownership of land by the Iron Age makes it unlikely that travellers were able to range freely across the landscape and that movement became channelled along defined, stock-proof trackways.

The map on page 74 illustrates accepted or likely prehistoric 'ways' in Lincolnshire. All were probably in existence as trackways before the Roman invasion, having emerged and been formalised at some point over the preceding four millennia. Together, they formed the core of a late prehistoric transport network for the movement of people, livestock and tradeable commodities, especially salt. Lesser pathways and droveways almost certainly also existed. Parts of this network were subsequently commandeered by the Romans (see next chapter), in some cases continuing as roads to the present day. Other parts have persisted as unsurfaced 'green lanes', of which Sewstern Lane is the best preserved overall.

The Jurassic Way: Lincolnshire's oldest road?

In Chapter 1, we saw how the escarpment of the Jurassic Oolites – the Lincoln Edge – forms a natural rampart running the length of Lincolnshire from the Leicestershire border to the Humber, with relatively minor breaks at the river gaps. There is little doubt that this had become important for prehistoric travel by the Neolithic period, if not earlier, and probably formed part of a long-distance route across southern Britain.

The idea of the Jurassic Way as a prehistoric trackway linking Somerset and Yorkshire was popular in the mid 20th century, when specific routes were postulated by linking up the archaeological sites known at the time. Subsequently, archaeologists have tended to see it more as a movement corridor than a single, defined trackway. There is no definitive evidence

FACING PAGE: **Lincoln Edge, Waddington.** The Lincoln Edge may once have been part of the Neolithic Jurassic Way, possibly as one of several strands of a braided or multiple route. Pottergate had probably emerged as a defined 'road' by the Iron Age. Today, this stretch of path is part of the Viking Way Long Distance Footpath.

either way, however, and the strongly linear topography of the Oolite escarpment in Lincolnshire suggests to the author that a more defined trackway is a distinct possibility here. North of Lincoln, Middle Street has long existed as a 'road' along the summit of the scarp to Scunthorpe; south of the city, the modern A606 and then Pottergate represent a possible route as far south as Ancaster. From here the route has left no trace but probably continued along or near the escarpment to Grantham, crossing or merging with the conjectural Salter's Way (see below) near Cold Harbour. Whether single, braided or multiple, the route between here and the River Welland is also speculative. It may have used the Salter's Way as far as Sewstern Lane, then followed the latter to Stamford. However, a direct route via the upper Witham and across Rutland to Stamford as a precursor to Ermine Street seems more likely. As noted above, sections of the Jurassic Way were either reused or bypassed by Roman roads, notably Ermine Street, with Middle Street and Pottergate apparently continuing as secondary highways.

Sewstern Lane: a prehistoric trackway under threat

Sewstern Lane is the best-preserved prehistoric trackway in Lincolnshire. Also known as the Drift, it runs today between Greetham (Rutland) and Long Bennington on the River Witham, and probably extended originally

Sewstern Lane scenes: near Denton (FACING PAGE), **near Wyville** (TOP RIGHT) **and near Allington** (RIGHT). Sewstern Lane forms much of the border between Lincolnshire and Leicestershire, hence its alternative local name The Mere, meaning boundary.

to a river crossing of the Trent near Newark (Notts). The continuation of the route as The Drift through Pickworth to the River Welland at Uffington appears to be of later date, as it cuts across Medieval parish boundaries.

Sewstern Lane is plausibly of Bronze Age vintage, as has long been mooted (Hoskins, 1955). This remains unsubstantiated, but the apparent Romanisation of the southern section of the route supports a prehistoric origin (Fisher, 2017). In Medieval times, it was an alternative to the Great North Road, with the latter winning out by the 17th century due to better servicing by urban centres. In later centuries it continued in use primarily as a drovers' road for cattle travelling to London from Scotland and northern England (see Chapter 14).

Today, parts of Sewstern Lane are a metalled road, but it remains an important historical landscape feature and is of high ecological value for its limestone flora where it crosses the Oolite plateau. Unfortunately, the rise of recreational off-roading has caused serious damage and disturbance to the unmetalled sections in recent years, and continues to be a problem despite legal restrictions on vehicle use introduced on some sections.

The Salter's Way & early salterns in Lincolnshire

The Salter's or Salt Way of Kesteven is often attributed to the Romans. Its generally accepted route is evidenced by road earthworks on Spittlegate Heath and the excavated Roman settlement at Saltersford on the River Witham near Grantham. Its likely continuation then followed the 'Roman' road across the Leicestershire Wolds to Six Hills and beyond. However, there are indications that the route may be older. Salt making has taken place on the Lincolnshire coast since at least the Bronze Age and continued with successive shifts in location and methods until the 1600s. The earliest archaeological evidence dates to the mid Bronze Age, with remains of salterns (salt making sites) identified at Tetney and Hogsthorpe in the Lindsey Marsh, at Stickford and along the Kesteven Fen Edge at Billingborough, Dowsby and south of Langtoft to Peterborough, mostly as 'briquetage' fragments buried by later wetland deposits (Lane, 2007). At this time, Lincolnshire's coastal zone of marshes and tidal creeks reached inland to the Fen Edges, thus providing the salterns with their source of brine.

Distribution of salt inland on trackways seems highly likely even at this early date, though the routes are speculative. For the Kesteven Fen Edge, it is probable that Mareham Lane – a 'Roman' road between Bourne and Sleaford – already existed as a route when the Bronze Age salterns were operating, and could have served these sites. It is also possible that the Salter's Way emerged at this time, especially as the generally accepted route runs inland from Bridge End on the Fen Edge – very close to the early salterns at Billingborough and Dowsby. The river crossing at Saltersford and continuation of the route into the Leicestershire Wolds past Saltby may therefore be pre-Roman too. Further north, the early salterns of Lindsey all had potential access to the prehistoric trackways of the Wolds for local if not wider distribution of salt.

In the Fen Basin, the subsequent expansion of peatland pushed Iron Age and Romano-British salt making (and settlement) progressively away

The existence of the Salter's Way before the Roman period is probable though unproven. The most likely route is that of the modern A52 from Bridge End – close to known Bronze Age and Iron Age salterns in the Kesteven Fens – to near Grantham. From Cold Harbour, there is a strongly suggestive alignment running south-west across the Witham valley at Saltersford and across the Leicestershire Wolds to Barrow-upon-Soar, following the 'Roman' road through Six Hills. Curiously, the village of Saltby, just inside Leicestershire, lies slightly south of this line and might indicate an alternative route. However, it must be remembered that villages like Saltby only became fixed in the Middle Anglo-Saxon period, two millennia after the earliest known salterns.

LEFT: **a possible route of the Salter's Way near Hungerton**. This quiet lane forms a crossroads with Sewstern Lane between Hungerton and Saltby (Leics) and also passes the prehistoric earthworks known as King Lud's Entrenchments (Leics).

from the Fen Edges towards the retreating coastline. This is illustrated by saltern sites in what is now drained fenland, as at Deeping Fen and Cowbit. These later sites were then also buried by peat development and silt from Fen rivers, but when active may have accessed pre-existing salt routes. Speculatively, the Bridge End Causeway which crosses the Fens to Donington may have originated as an extension of the Salter's Way. If so, the latter conceivably remained in continuous use for moving salt from the Bronze Age until Romano-British times and later served the Medieval salt industry around Bicker Haven. Another fen causeway, the Baston Outgang, was probably built to access salterns and settlements in the Spalding area, but is generally attributed to the Roman period. Other likely causeway routes across the Fens, such as the Hill Dyke Causeway between Sibsey and Boston, have not so far been linked specifically with salterns, and probably developed as more general routes in early Medieval times (see Chapter 13).

Wolds ways: Caistor High Street, the Bluestone Heath Road and Barton Street

The prehistoric 'ways' of the Lincolnshire Wolds share several features with those of the Jurassic Oolite ridge. They have likely origins as trackways predating the Roman conquest, and were later upgraded to form part of the Roman road network. Similarly, they follow strongly linear courses near the eastern and western limits of the uplands. The classic example is Caistor High Street, often described as a Roman road linking the fort settlements of *Bannovallum* (Horncastle) and Caistor, but almost certainly representing an earlier route along the escarpment of the Wolds that extended to the Humber. Today, it is a metalled road, the B1225, still known as High Street between Baumber and Caistor. It passes several Bronze Age tumuli and a Neolithic long barrow near Normanby Top.

The Bluestone Heath Road is surely the most romantically named of Lincolnshire's prehistoric ways. It once ran from the southern limit of the Wolds, possibly near Burgh-le-Marsh, climbing the high ridges of the Wolds to join High Street near Ludford. Parts of it were subsequently Romanised, particularly the section between Candlesby and Ulceby, which formed the main road between Roman Lincoln and the coast. However, the highest

FACING PAGE: **view east from Caistor High Street, near Otby**

RIGHT: **snowdrift in track, Risby Top**

71

section from Driby northwards was bypassed by the Romans, and survives today as a secondary road as far as Calcethorpe.

The age of the Bluestone Heath Road is uncertain. Described by some as a 'Celtic' – presumably Iron Age – droveway, it could equally be a much older route given the abundant evidence of Neolithic and Bronze Age activity in the Wolds. The name is thought to derive from erratic boulders known as 'bluestones' which were deposited on the Wolds by glaciers.

The third main Wolds 'way' is Barton Street, which ran along the foot of the former cliffline adjoining the Lindsey Marshland between Burgh-le-Marsh and Barton-upon-Humber. The northern section corresponds to the A18 and other modern roads between Laceby and Barton. South of Louth there is no clear physical survival and the specific line is uncertain. By the Iron Age at the latest, it is likely to have connected to well-established estuary crossing points at the Humber and Wash respectively, the latter linking to the north Norfolk coast near Hunstanton.

72

TOP LEFT: **sunset near Maidenwell, Wolds**

LEFT: **Bronze Age round barrow near Tathwell, Wolds**

FACING PAGE: **chalk landscape near Worlaby**

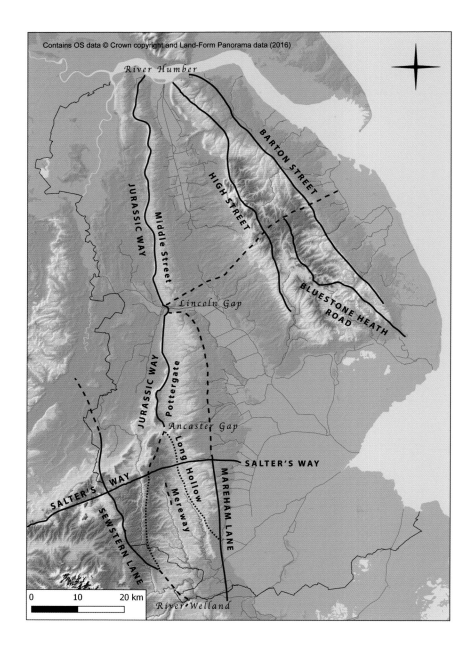

Contains OS data © Crown copyright and Land-Form Panorama data (2016)

74

Prehistoric Trackways in Lincolnshire

— probable trackway of Iron Age or earlier origin

– – ditto, but route less certain

- - - - other possible trackway as suggested in this book

Parts of the following trackways are thought to have been reused and upgraded during the Roman occupation (see map on page 86):

- Bluestone Heath Road

- High Street

- Jurassic Way (*Middle Street, Pottergate and possibly Ermine Street between the River Welland and Ancaster*)*

- Long Hollow (*King Street*)

- Mareham Lane

- Sewstern Lane (*Greetham to Three Queens*)

* the Jurassic Way is thought to have crossed the River Welland close to what is now Stamford town centre, east of the ford created subsequently by the Romans for Ermine Street. However, Ermine Street may have utilised the existing Jurassic Way between Stamford and Greetham (Rutland), and possibly also northwards on a conjectural route along the upper Witham valley to Spittlegate Heath and Ancaster

Source: May (1976) plus information from Fisher (2017) and Stocker (2003)

References

Fisher, P.J. (2017), *Buckminster and Sewstern*, The Victoria County History of Leicestershire

Hoskins, W.G. (1955), *The Making of the English Landscape*, Hodder & Stoughton

Lane, T., *'Until the Seas Boil Dry': Landscape and Salt in Bronze Age Lincolnshire* in Howard, J. & Start, D. (eds) (2007), *All Things Lincolnshire*, Society for Lincolnshire History & Archaeology

Malone, S., *Making Tracks*, in Howard, J. & Lester, C. (eds) (2005), *Lincolnshire on the Move*, Society for Lincolnshire History & Archaeology

May, J. (1976), *Prehistoric Lincolnshire*, History of Lincolnshire Committee, Lincoln

Stocker, D. (ed) (2003), *The City by the Pool*, Oxbow Books

RIGHT: **evening sunrays near the Mereway, Kesteven Uplands**

5 : ROMAN ENGINEERING
A Legacy of Roads & Canals?

In the last chapter, we saw how a network of trackways had developed across Lincolnshire by later prehistoric times, transporting people, livestock and commodities, above all salt. Archaeological remains of ancient boats in Lincolnshire clearly show that movement by water was also well established by the Bronze Age and probably earlier. This chapter looks at the impact of the Roman occupation on these transport routes, focusing on the evidence for engineered roads and canals surviving in the modern landscape.

Revolution or makeover: what did the Romans actually do for transport in Britain?

Until recently, British historians of the Roman period generally presented the Roman conquest as a culturally beneficent development which brought Classical civilisation, literacy, urbanism and central government – as well as vastly improved transport infrastructure – to Britain. In this view, peaking in the 19th and early 20th centuries, a primitive Iron Age culture of warring British tribes living in 'huts' and hill forts gave way to stone architecture

in towns connected by an efficient new road network, plus assorted other advances such as writing, numeracy, sanitation, villa living and so on. However, this establishment perspective with its pro-Roman cultural bias has been giving way to more critical and nuanced interpretations in recent decades. In our own post-imperial era, the Roman occupation is seen more as colonialism which ruthlessly exploited the people, land and resources of Britain as an imperial possession (Mattingly, 2006). Moreover, the notion of an abrupt and dramatic pre-Roman to Roman cultural leap forward is

FACING PAGE: **Tillbridge Lane at the Lincoln Edge, Scampton**

RIGHT: **High Dyke (Ermine Street) crossing Lincoln Heath, Fulbeck**

78

also waning, with archaeology revealing Britain in the late Iron Age as an advanced agricultural society that was already being drawn into the orbit of the Roman 'superpower' before the actual invasion of AD 43. Increasingly, continuities of lifestyle, settlement location, field layouts and technology between Iron Age and Roman Britain are becoming apparent, especially for ordinary Britons living in the prosperous lowland country-side of south-eastern Britain, including Lincolnshire.

So, where does this leave us on Roman roads? Should they still be viewed as a heroic programme of new highways that transformed a Britain of inchoate, muddy ways and bequeathed a legacy of strategic routes which are still in use today? Or, was it more a makeover of a pre-existing network, the latter being much more extensive and better engineered than has previously been realised? Despite the paucity of historical evidence relating to actual road building in Roman Britain, there is no real doubt that the Romans

FACING PAGE: **Mareham Lane, Aswarby / Scredington.** Mareham Lane runs along the Kesteven Fen Edge between the Roman settlements of Bourne and Sleaford. Like many routes attributed to the Romans, however, it is likely to be pre-Roman in origin. A continuation of the road north to Lincoln is thought to correspond to Bloxholm Lane.

RIGHT: **Newport Arch, Lincoln.** This is the best-preserved of Lincoln's Roman gateways. Here, Ermine Street passed through the Roman city's northern defensive wall heading north for the Humber crossing at Winteringham. A succession of Roman road surfaces and repairs has been revealed by various excavations on Ermine Street in Lincolnshire, while the Roman *agger* still forms a visible feature in places, notably as High Dyke between Ancaster and Byard's Leap and on the A15 north of Lincoln.

generally engineered their roads to a high standard. This included the construction of a raised causeway (*agger*), lateral drainage ditches and two-layered metalling of stone and sand or gravel. Bridges and culverts were added to cross rivers and streams. Likewise, Roman surveyors were obviously capable of creating straight courses over long distances, linking directly the new military and urban centres.

However, archaeology is now challenging even the established view that Roman road planning and construction were fundamentally different from anything seen previously in Britain (and then not equalled until the 18th century). Evidence of a carefully engineered Iron Age road with lateral bounding banks and a cambered and cobbled surface has recently been discovered at Sharpstone Hill in Shropshire, dating originally to 200 BC, over two centuries before the Roman conquest (*Pryor, 2014). Known as the Portway, this was used for transporting heavy loads between the Midlands and the ore mining areas of the Welsh Borders. A metalled track has also been found in Yorkshire (Bishop, 2014). Comparable engineering has not so far been identified in Lincolnshire but, as seen in Chapter 4, the prehistoric transport network here included routes that were certainly of regional if not wider significance for movement and trade. Survivals such as Sewstern Lane also indicate the existence of defined trackways running on a direct if not course over long distances, suggesting that prehistoric Britons possessed surveying skills.

Rather than always building anew, it seems likely that the Romans often commandeered existing routes – possibly even surfaced roads – albeit that these may have been upgraded. In Lincolnshire, Caistor High Street and Mareham Lane have long been placed in this category, but other 'Roman' roads probably existed before the conquest, with the Salter's Way and King Street being prime candidates. Much of Ermine Street can probably still be regarded as a new Roman road built for rapid military access, bypassing the older Jurassic Way. However, the author would not be surprised if Britain's trackways were already being metalled for wheeled transport by the late Iron Age and were simply upgraded by the Romans. Perhaps we even need to revisit the discredited ideas of Alfred Watkins (1922), at least on the use of sight lines or 'leys' in the creation of prehistoric trackways.

Roads in Roman Lincolnshire

At the time of the Roman invasion, the Lincolnshire area lay within the lands of the *Corieltauvi* people, who came relatively quickly under Roman control before AD 50. The Roman army established early forts at Lincoln and Newton-on-Trent for military consolidation and further advance into northern England. The major legionary fortress on the Lincoln hilltop dates to the AD 60s, possibly in response to the Boudican Revolt, and subsequently gave way to a colony for retired army veterans in the early AD 90s, named *Lindum Colonia*. Later, in the 4th century, Lincoln became the provincial capital of either *Flavia Caesariensis* or *Britannia Secunda* within the Romano-British diocese, one of four such provinces in Britain.

The network of roads in Roman Lincolnshire was therefore focused on Lincoln from the outset (see map on page 86), albeit that this may ultimately reflect the pre-Roman importance of this location as a river crossing point

The roads of Roman Lincolnshire vary considerably in the extent and nature of their preservation today. Some routes including Ermine Street, the Fosse Way, Mareham Lane and Tillbridge Lane remained in use and have been wholly or partly incorporated into the modern road network. Conversely, other routes only exist archaeologically as former courses without being visible on the surface, such as most of King Street between Bourne and Ancaster. Some routes declined in importance historically, but are still used by minor roads, green lanes or tracks. Only the place element 'street' is derived from the Romans – lane, gate and dyke are all later words.

King Street branched off Ermine Street at the Roman settlement of *Durobrivae* west of Peterborough, running northwards through Bourne and Sapperton to rejoin Ermine Street on Wilsford Heath near Ancaster. Little survives of the route north of Bourne, though short sections remain as lanes and tracks, as **near Sapperton** (RIGHT). There is a roughly parallel 'way' from **Long Hollow near Oasby** (BOTTOM RIGHT) across Wilsford Heath to the Ancaster Valley that strongly suggests a pre-Roman precursor to King Street.

and spiritual focus. From Lincoln, roads radiated in several directions, the principal ones being Ermine Street (London to Lincoln and the Humber) and the Fosse Way (Exeter to Lincoln via Bath, Cirencester and Leicester). North of Lincoln, Tillbridge Lane branched off Ermine Street to the Trent crossing at *Segelocum* (Littleborough, Notts). An inscribed Roman milestone relating to the latter route is held in The Collection in Lincoln. Another road headed west from Lincoln to the coast, probably connecting to a ferry crossing over the Wash to Norfolk. Elsewhere

within Lincolnshire, key routes included Caistor High Street, King Street, Mareham Lane and the Kesteven Salter's Way. Also associated with salt production is Baston Outgang, which has been traced across the Fens from Baston to Spalding, and would have provided access to the numerous Romano-British settlements and salterns hereabouts. In addition to these main routes, there were almost certainly numerous smaller roads and tracks, many probably of pre-Roman origin, serving the scatttered rural settlements and farms of the countryside.

Car Dyke and the Fossdyke: a Roman canal system?

If archaeology is raising questions about the origin of Roman roads, the situation with Roman canals in Lincolnshire is yet more uncertain. The current edition of the Ordnance Survey's *Roman Britain* map still shows both Car Dyke and the Fossdyke as artificial watercourses designed for drainage and/or transport, clearly implying that both are of Roman origin. Of the two, Car Dyke is now less impressive physically but perhaps the more intriguing archaeologically. Its state of preservation varies but it can be traced for some 57 miles (92km) between Peterborough and Washingborough near Lincoln. The waterway follows the Fen Edge

82

TOP LEFT: **pedestrian entrance, Newport Arch, Lincoln**

LEFT: **Fossdyke canal near Lincoln**

FACING PAGE: **Brayford Pool, Lincoln**

and probably extended to the River Witham at Lincoln. Curiously, the central portion between Market Deeping and Billinghay is largely straight whereas the two end portions are much more sinuous, suggesting that it may not have been constructed as a single project. Evidence of branch canals exists at Rippingale and between Bourne and Morton Fen.

Car Dyke has generally been attributed to the Romans since its recognition as an ancient monument by the antiquarian John Morton in the early 18th century. However, evidence for Roman construction remains circumstantial, and a late Iron Age or post-Roman origin cannot be ruled out. The purpose of Car Dyke also remains uncertain, though most scholars today favour it being a catchwater drain rather than a canal as once thought, albeit that some local transport may have occurred. One appealing if unproven suggestion is that the Romans operated the central section of Car Dyke between Bourne and Sleaford in conjunction with a second, outer drain corresponding to the Medieval *Midfendic* – these two drains being connected by canalised 'lodes' and controlling the transfer of water from the uplands of Kesteven to the sea (Simmons & Cope-Faulkner, 2004). Recently, some writers have suggested that Car Dyke was the boundary of a Roman imperial estate which controlled salt production in the Fens.

The Fossdyke is a navigable waterway running between Brayford Pool in Lincoln and the River Trent at Torksey. Unlike Car Dyke, it is and has probably always functioned as a canal. Historical sources indicate that it was recut in the 12th century following an earlier but silted course. The latter is often attributed to the Romans but could equally have been post-Roman. Indeed, the archaeology around Brayford Pool suggests a possible Anglo-Danish origin, particularly as the main docks for Roman Lincoln apparently lay on the River Witham to the east of the walled city rather than on Brayford Pool as once believed (Jones, 2014). Periodic improvements to the Fossdyke were made in the post-Medieval centuries, including a navigable sluice or tidal lock at Torksey in 1672. After further silting problems, the canal was redredged in the 1740s, greatly boosting Lincoln's trade and economy. The banks of the Fossdyke were heightened in the early 19th century in connection with Sir John Rennie the Elder's drainage scheme for the fens west of Lincoln (Stocker, 2003).

To conclude the chaper, what then is the legacy of Roman transport engineering in the landscape of Lincolnshire? Clearly, there has been a tendency to attribute features to Roman rather than native endeavour, affecting both prehistoric and post-Roman remains. Simultaneously, there is now increasing evidence that Iron Age Britons knew how to lay out straight roads and to engineer and surface these for wheeled transport. The extent to which the Romans actually transformed Britain with a new network of engineered roads has thus been called into question. In Lincolnshire, several roads ascribed unambiguously to the Roman period lack definitive evidence for such and some, at least, are almost certainly of earlier origin and were simply reused by the Roman invaders. The case for Roman construction of Car Dyke and the Fossdyke Canal remains moot.

FACING PAGE: **Car Dyke at Swaton, Kesteven Fen Edge**

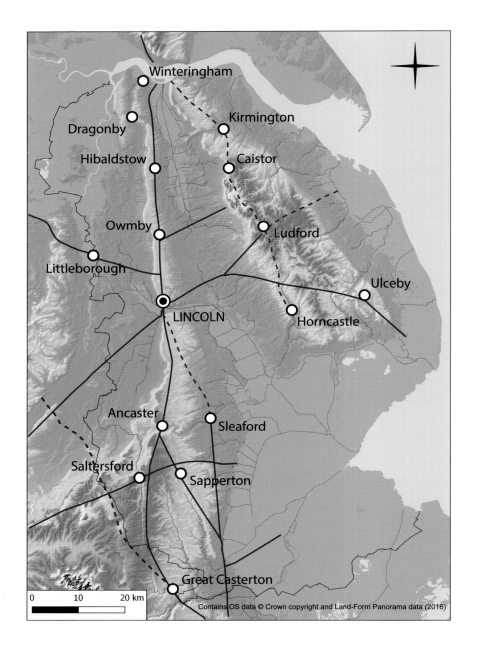

Roads in Roman Lincolnshire

——— main roads - physical survival and/or other strong evidence

– – – main roads - probable

◉ major Roman town

○ other main Roman settlement

Winteringham

Dragonby

Kirmington

Hibaldstow

Caistor

Owmby

Ludford

Littleborough

Ulceby

LINCOLN

Horncastle

Ancaster

Sleaford

Saltersford

Sapperton

Great Casterton

0　10　20 km

Contains OS data © Crown copyright and Land-Form Panorama data (2016)

Source: Lee (2016) and Stocker (2003)

References

Bishop, M.C. (2014), *The Secret History of the Roman Roads of Britain*, Pen & Sword, Barnsley

Jones, M.J. (2011), *Roman Lincoln: Conquest, Colony & Capital*, The History Press, Stroud

Jones, M.J., *The Archaeology of Brayford Pool* in Walker, A. (ed) (2014), *Brayford Pool: Lincoln's Waterfront Through Time*, The Survey of Lincoln

Lee, A. (2016), *Treasures of Roman Lincolnshire*, Amberley Publishing, Stroud

Mattingly, D. (2006), *An Imperial Possession: Britain in the Roman Empire, 54 BC - AD 409*, Penguin Books

Simmons, B.B. & Cope-Faulkner, P. (2004), *The Car Dyke*, Lincolnshire Archaeology and Heritage Reports Series No 8, Heritage Trust of Lincolnshire, Heckington

Stocker, D. (ed) (2003), *The City by the Pool*, Oxbow Books

Watkins, A. (1922), *Early British Trackways*, Hereford & London

RIGHT: the 'Roman' road to the coast, Hemingby

6 : FIELD & FURROW
Farming Patterns from the Past

Fields are perhaps the most significant man-made element in Lincolnshire's countryside. Their size, boundaries and patterns are still central to the varied character of the rural landscape, whilst also reflecting historical changes in agriculture dating back at least to the Romano-British period. This chapter explores fields in Lincolnshire up to Medieval times, focusing on their boundaries and other lines surviving in the landscape today. The next chapter picks up the story from the 14th century, when the enclosure of the landscape into private fields using hedges or walls began in earnest.

Early agriculture and the emergence of fields

When settlers brought agriculture to Britain from continental Europe just before 4000 BC, they also introduced two new and related features to the landscape – the cultivation plot and the stockproof barrier. These have continued to evolve within the changing cultural and technological context of the countryside up to the present day, and now correspond essentially to farmers' fields and field boundaries. Today, archaeology is revealing the long history of fields back to their beginnings.

FACING PAGE: **buttercups showing ridge and furrow, Saxby All Saints, Wolds**

RIGHT: **relict open field landscape, Haxey, Isle of Axholme**

Until recently, it was thought that agriculture spread very slowly across Britain, perhaps over two millennia, with early agriculturalists in England living transitionally as mobile livestock herders practising 'slash and burn' agriculture on temporary cultivation plots. Such lifestyles cannot be ruled out entirely, but new archaeological work is fundamentally challenging this established model. Improved dating has shown that the adoption of agriculture throughout Britain took a mere 200 years, reaching northern Scotland by c. 3800 BC. Manuring is now known to have been a part of

The earliest fields identified so far in Lincolnshire date to the Bronze Age. Located along the Welland valley and Kesteven Fen Edge, these early field systems were primarily for livestock farming of sheep and cattle. Consisting of fields, droveways and houses, they are now visible only as crop marks. However, archaeological excavation at Welland Bank Quarry and Flag Fen (Peterborough) has revealed highly valuable information about farming in the Bronze Age and Iron Age.

90

LEFT: **reconstructed Bronze Age dwelling, Flag Fen, Peterborough.** The Flag Fen site lies on the edge of the Fens just south of Lincolnshire, but its Bronze Age field systems are broadly similar to those found in south Kesteven. Originally laid out around 2500 BC, some fields and droveways have been recreated here using plant species present in the Bronze Age pollen record. The thatched dwelling is a reconstruction of one excavated nearby at Fengate dating to c. 3100 BC.

FACING PAGE: **flock of Hebridean sheep, Crowle Moor.** 'Primitive' breeds such as the Soay and Hebridean are the closest relatives to Britain's prehistoric sheep.

the agricultural 'package' imported into Britain, allowing permanent cultivation without soil depletion. Furthermore, archaeologists are finding more and more sites of permanent settlement from the Mesolithic period, showing that some, maybe most, of Britain's hunter-gatherers lived in static villages well before agriculture arrived. Remarkably, the earliest such sites date to c. 9000 BC, a mere 700 years after the final (Loch Lomond) cold snap of the Ice Age ended. A new conception of early agriculture is therefore emerging, in which domesticated livestock and crops slotted relatively easily and quickly into existing, settled landscapes that were already intensively managed for prey species and plant resources (*Pryor, 2014). The earliest cultivation in Lincolnshire probably occurred around 6,000 years ago in small plots adjoining the village settlements or

houses of Neolithic livestock farmers, growing cereals and possibly fruit and nuts too. The use of stockproof barriers, probably hedges, around these early cultivation plots seems almost certain if so far unproven.

Despite this picture, the emergence of more complex field systems has not yet been pushed back earlier than the Bronze Age in Britain (cf. the earliest known field systems in Ireland date to c. 3500 BC). Nationally, the finest upstanding examples are perhaps the rectilinear grids of field-banks or 'reaves' seen on Dartmoor, beautifully preserved due to upland abandonment in the deteriorating climate of the Iron Age. However, fields that were definitely in use in the Bronze Age have been identified in Lincolnshire, surviving as crop or soil marks in the modern landscape.

Some of the most significant sites are in the Welland valley and Kesteven Fen Edge, where highly organised field systems for livestock emerged adjoining the developing fen wetlands. Crop marks here include ditched fields, droveways, stockyards and dispersed settlements of roundhouses, though these features are not necessarily all contemporaneous (*Pryor, 2014).

Probably of slightly later date, crop marks of linear earthworks suggest that Lincolnshire's Jurassic uplands had been brought into farming use by the later Iron Age (Bewley, 1998). The date and purpose of these features are difficult to interpret, but multiple-ditched earthworks on and near the Oolite ridge may have been territorial boundaries and/or access trackways. It is unclear whether farming here was arable or pastoral at this time.

Fields of Britannia: an inheritance from the Romano-British countryside?

On the eve of the Roman invasion of Britain, most landscape historians and archaeologists agree, Lincolnshire already had a prosperous, farmed countryside of open character, dominated by fields and small, scattered farmsteads and farming settlements, probably denser in Kesteven than in Lindsey. Overall, the impact of the Roman conquest on this countryside appears to have been one of modification and intensification rather than wholesale change. Farming innovations were introduced, including new technology (heavy plough, scythe) and new crops (cabbage, parsnip, turnip, carrot, celery, plum, apple and, probably, vine). Later in the Romano-British period, the villa became more common as a feature of the landscape,

and agriculture focused increasingly on wheat and beef production for the market economy. However, much of the farmed countryside probably altered little, and some earlier, prehistoric fields may even have persisted through the Roman occupation.

So, does anything survive of the Romano-British fieldscape today? Unlike some parts of England, there are no known Lincolnshire examples of Romano-British or earlier field systems with their earthworks upstanding. It used to be thought that the cultivation terraces seen in the Wolds were ancient, preserved by their hillside location, but these are now known to be Medieval. However, like their predecessors, Romano-British field systems have left crop marks and buried archaeology, notably as ditches. Evidence was once sparse outside the Fens, but excavation is now revealing Roman fields across Lincolnshire. Typically, these follow a pattern seen in the East Midlands of rectangular fields in blocks divided by roads and trackways.

Until recently, evidence suggested that the laying out of Medieval open fields ignored the pre-existing field patterns, including any Romano-British or earlier survivals. However, new research (Rippon, 2015) is pointing to widespread continuity of orientation and/or boundaries between Romano-British and Medieval fields, even in open-field areas like Lincolnshire. Furthermore, where the subsequent enclosure of open fields occurred prior to the Parliamentary phase (see next chapter), this often perpetuated the same ancient orientations and boundaries. It is only where Parliamentary enclosure took place, imposing a surveyor's layout wholly unrelated to the open fields, that continuity was necessarily lost. Thus, Lincolnshire parishes enclosed before c. 1750 may contain historic field patterns that can be

traced back to Romano-British times and potentially even earlier. The main area where this is not seen is the Fens, as marine silts and/or fen peat buried much of the Romano-British land surface here, creating a new canvas for Medieval and later field layouts.

One possible feature of the Romano-British landscape that remains elusive is 'centuriation' – a Roman system of surveying which divided areas into

ABOVE: **cultivation terraces, Binbrook, Lincolnshire Wolds.** These terraces or 'strip lynchets' are one of several such sites in the Wolds, including Gaumer Hill, The Lofts (Scamblesby Thorpe) and Caistor. Once ascribed to the Roman period as possible vineyards – the pictured site lies close to a Roman villa – they are now generally considered to be of Medieval date and were cultivated as part of open-field agriculture. Outside of the Wolds, the only strip lynchets in Lincolnshire known to the author are feint, probable remains on the Lincoln Edge at Burton / South Carlton. However, they do occur at Croxton Kerrial and Knipton (Leics) very near the Kesteven border.

an extensive grid of squares or rectangles (*centuriae*) for land allocation and the laying out of new roads, forts and other features. The planned, geometric landscapes of centuriation can still be seen in parts of the Mediterranean, but possible British examples remain controversial. Perhaps the most plausible area in Lincolnshire lies in the Fens north of Peterborough, where some roads, settlements and waterways appear to correspond to a potential centuriation grid. Another area requiring further investigation is Lincoln itself, where land surrounding the *Colonia* is highly likely to have been parcelled out for retired army veterans.

Medieval fields: open fields and strip farming

If time travel becomes possible, a visit to the Medieval countryside will surely rank a close second to that of prehistoric or Roman times. In 1300, most of Lincolnshire outside the Fens and Marshland had a 'champion' countryside of compact villages surrounded by their open fields. In the vales especially, the unenclosed fieldscape of arable strips was punctuated only by occasional hedges, scattered trees and meadow along the brooks and

becks. In autumn and spring, teams of oxen up to eight strong ploughed the strips under vast Lincolnshire skies, creating the ridge and furrow pattern that is still visible today in old pastures. Essentially, it is the lost landscape of the Northamptonshire poet John Clare in its Medieval heyday, before enclosure began to transform the countryside back into private fields and farms.

Open-field agriculture had itself involved a major reshaping of the landscape, especially in the so-called Central Region – the broad swathe running diagonally across England from Somerset to Yorkshire. Here, villages developed in the Anglo-Saxon period through a process of settlement stabilisation and convergence known as 'nucleation', and open fields replaced the previous field systems, albeit sometimes respecting their orientation or boundaries. Whether these changes occurred by evolution

95

Several parishes in the Isle of Axholme retained open fields as part of their Enclosure awards in the 19th century. Today, despite the amalgamation of farming strips, this is the largest area of relict open field landscape in England, and probably the best place to appreciate the lost 'champion' countryside which dominated the Midlands before enclosure. These scenes show relict strips at **Epworth** (FACING PAGE) and **Belton Field** (RIGHT). Sadly, a conservation scheme which recreated strip planting elsewhere in the former open fields has recently been discontinued while new funding is sought.

Medieval field earthworks are probably the earliest to have survived as upstanding features in the present-day landscape in Lincolnshire. Best known is the 'corrugated' pattern of former strips known as ridge and furrow (rig and furrow in Lincolnshire dialect), which is preserved in old pasture in many parts of the county. Sometimes the furlong boundaries can also be seen, as here at **Burton-by-Lincoln** (LEFT). Ridge and furrow was created by ploughing the soil into ridges to improve drainage, especially on heavier clay soils. It is absent from East Anglia, where 'flat ploughing' was practised, and appears to have been rare in the Fens, where flat-topped 'dylings' were used. Not all surviving ridge and furrow is of Medieval date, as open-field layouts were frequently altered or extended in later centuries. The practice of ploughing into cultivation ridges also continued until the improvement of field underdrainage from the 1830s, even occurring in enclosed fields. Late ridges are straight, whereas earlier ridge and furrow typically shows a slightly curved, 'reversed S' form which reduced the space needed for plough teams to turn at the headlands.

or as a single 'replanning' is still debated, along with their timing. However, there is a degree of consensus that open-field farming emerged in the Central Region in the 8th or 9th century, probably after nucleation, with the initial laying out of open fields continuing up to the Norman Conquest or shortly after. In any case, by the Domesday Survey of 1086, Lincolnshire's uplands, vales, Fen Edges and Middle Marsh had acquired the full complement of villages that exist today – as well as others which later failed – and a strip-based farming system which operated in some parishes for over 1,000 years.

Open-field agriculture continued to evolve, but its key elements endured. The basic unit of cultivation was a strip called a 'land'. These were grouped lengthwise into a block or 'furlong', and the furlongs arranged in a loose, chequerboard pattern to form a 'field'. Each village or 'township' operated two – later often three or four – such fields, which were the basis of communal farming operations. Individuals owned or rented a number of strips according to their wealth and social status, but holdings were scattered throughout the furlongs and were subject to a fixed crop rotation and common grazing and fallowing, all under the control of a manorial court. The lord and church had holdings called the *demesne* and *glebe*.

While open fields dominate our view of the Medieval countryside, they were one element of a system which integrated all of a township's land resources, including meadow, pasture, woodland and rough commons. Unlike some 'champion' areas, Lincolnshire townships usually possessed ample grassland, with meadowland along wetland margins and grazing on unreclaimed fenland and heathland. The village meadow was also divided into strips ('doles'), though, unlike the ridged 'lands', these have left no physical trace today. Medieval farming in Lincolnshire also varied with local conditions and soils, each parish reflecting its own particular geography. In the chalk Wolds, the village arable was limited in extent and parishes were dominated by extensive, unenclosed 'heath' (Williamson, 2004). Here, large flocks of sheep were grazed by day and folded on the arable at night, thereby improving the light soils with their dung – a system of 'sheep-corn' husbandry found in other chalklands and the Cotswolds.

The Fens and Lindsey Marsh followed different paths from the 'champion' areas in their Medieval farming and field patterns, albeit that both also had strip-based systems. Conceivably, the primary settlements of the Townlands around the Wash may initially have had large open fields but, if so, these were superseded by the numerous small, irregular-shaped fields seen today.

TOP RIGHT: **manor house, church and farmstead in the village, Sapperton**

RIGHT: **sheep on rough pasture in the Wolds, Thoresway**

98

Blocks of parallel, elongated fields were then added by reclamation from the adjoining saltmarsh and fen. Fields were subdivided into strip holdings, for which the flat, ditched form called 'dylings' seems to have been usual (Hall, 2014). Dylings provided drainage and were still being created in the early 1800s. Fenland strips were superficially like open-field 'lands' but had looser tenurial patterns and fewer controls. Many Medieval field boundaries still exist despite amalgamation, but survivals of dylings are extremely rare.

In the Lindsey Outmarsh, the seasonal settlements established by salter-graziers developed into separate parishes with their own distinctive field systems. Typically, these consisted of elongated holdings ('dales') created by the division of wetland commons, often split later into sections, and used flexibly for arable and/or meadow (Gardiner, 2009). Ridging was usual when ploughing and is still preserved widely as earthworks in old pasture.

Except in the Isle of Axholme, Lincolnshire's Medieval fields were enclosed from later Medieval times onwards, yet features from the Medieval – and possibly earlier – farmed landscape persist. Even in the former open-field areas, these include old hedgelines, tracks and paths, as well as earthwork remains of open fields, woodbanks and deserted villages. In the former wetlands, many more Medieval field boundaries survive as reedy dykes and/or hedges. The more one looks, the more of the Medieval landscape is still visible, only partially obscured by later changes.

98

Patterns of Medieval farming in the wetlands: dylings preserved in pasture, **Donington, Fens** (TOP LEFT) and a long field or 'dole' at **Saltfleetby, Lindsey Outmarsh** (LEFT).

References

Bewley, R.H. (ed.)(1998), *Lincolnshire's Archaeology from the Air*, Society for Lincolnshire History & Archaeology

Gardiner, M. (2009), *Dales, long lands and the medieval division of land in eastern England*, The Agicultural History Review, Volume 57, Number 1

Hall, D. (2014), *The Open Fields of England*, Oxford University Press

Plaxton, S. and Graham, T. (2015), *Landscape Conservation Action Plan*, Isle of Axholme and Hatfield Chase Landscape Partnership

Rippon, S. et al (2015), *The Fields of Britannia: Continuity and Change in the Late Roman and Early Medieval Landscape*, Oxford University Press

Russell, R. (1995), *The Logic of Open Field Systems*, Society for Lincolnshire History & Archaeology

Williamson, T. (2004), *Shaping Medieval Landscapes*, Windgather

RIGHT: **old field dyke, Saltfleetby St. Peter, Lindsey Outmarsh**

7 : HEDGES & WALLS
A Living Record of Enclosure

The last chapter traced the story of fields in the Lincolnshire landscape up to the Medieval period, focusing on the legacy of relict earthworks and field boundaries in the modern countryside. This chapter picks up the story from around 1350, when it becomes increasingly linked to that of hedges and walls, as the process of enclosing farmland began in earnest. However, it is worth noting that fields bounded by hedges or walls had existed well before this period, certainly in the Bronze Age and probably earlier. These earlier, 'pre-enclosure' hedges are briefly considered here too.

Not all hedges and walls are related to farming activities, but their main functions have always been to contain or exclude grazing livestock and to define or emphasise property boundaries. Today, they are generally regarded as attractive and ecologically beneficial landscape features that warrant conservation, together with the associated craft traditions of hedgelaying and drystone walling. However, they also embody the history of the countryside relating to enclosure, which was socially controversial and destructive of many important wildlife habitats including heathland and fenland. Hedges, especially, reflect wider developments in British

history in their form and ecology, evolving as the countryside underwent successive change from the late peasant world through to our own era.

Hedges before the Enclosures: closes, assarts and more

The origin of hedges in Lincolnshire is necessarily speculative as elsewhere. It is possible that hedges emerged accidentally from early 'brushwood' barriers or hurdles that took root and sprouted. Certainly, by the Bronze

FACING PAGE: **hedgerow with beech trees, Stainton-le-Vale, Wolds**

RIGHT: **drystone wall detail and farm buildings, Normanton Heath**

LEFT: **wall on parish boundary of Normanton and Sudbrook, Lincoln Heath.** Lincolnshire's surviving field, road and parish boundary walls are generally assumed to date from the 1800s or later. However, there is archaeological evidence of drystone walling in Lincolnshire from the Roman period at Winterton, and the potential for pre-Parliamentary enclosure walls in the landscape warrants further study. Is it possible that Medieval or earlier boundary walls persist, especially on the Heath or Cliff?

Age, hedges of blackthorn were already being planted and layed at Flag Fen (Peterborough) in connection with droveways and fields for livestock farming on the Fen Edge, as shown by preserved 'pleachers' dated by radio carbon to 2500 BC (*Pryor, 2010). There is no reason to suppose this site was unique, so hedges were probably a feature in Lincolnshire by that date too. The use of hedges clearly continued through the succeeding Iron Age and Roman periods, though they are generally evidenced archaeologically only where combined with ditches. It is therefore uncertain how enclosed the drier areas of Lincolnshire were in these periods. Whether there is

any physical continuity from early hedges to the present is very doubtful given the repeated alteration of the farmed landscape over the centuries. However, it is a bold archaeologist who claims there can be no hedgeline of Roman or even prehistoric origin lurking somewhere in Lincolnshire!

By the later Anglo-Saxon period, much of Lincolnshire was developing the classic 'champion' landscape based on mature open-field agriculture, becoming more open in character than at any other time in its farming history. However, the Medieval farmed landscape was not without hedges even at the zenith of the open fields. 'Closes' – small, private fields for livestock and horses – developed around the village centres from the outset, and private enclosures were also being made by direct clearance from woodland and heathland throughout the Medieval period – a process known as 'assarting'. Similarly, along the wetland margins, private closes were being created (as well as common meadows), as seen along the Fen Edges and on the lower slopes of the 'island' of the Isle of Axholme. Even in the classic 'champion' areas of the clay vales, with their large open fields, there is evidence that hedges were used to mark parish boundaries, and to protect the arable and hay meadow from livestock as required. Trees were widely planted in such hedges for timber and pollarding (Williamson, 2017). Meanwhile, in the reclaimed siltlands of the Townlands and Lindsey Marsh, the Medieval fields were usually ditched, but some may also have had hedges to control stock, especially along droveways. Certainly, the process of enclosing 'open' (i.e. communally-farmed) land began earlier here than in the 'champion' districts, and free peasants may well have hedged their private holdings against their neighbours' stock.

What are the Enclosures and why did they happen?

At its simplest, enclosure means to surround an area of land with a hedge or wall, thereby creating a 'close'. However, in English social and landscape history, it has a further meaning relating to the form of tenure in which

RIGHT: **hedgelaying within the village today, Brant Broughton**

the land is held. Specifically, enclosure also describes the legal process whereby land was transferred from open-field arable, meadow, pasture and rough common, to private land held in severalty by a single owner, with all previous rights of other parties extinguished. Essentially, it meant that owners and tenants were no longer subject to communal access to their land for grazing or other purposes, and were also free to farm it however they chose. Hedges and walls were thus the physical manifestation of a redistribution of land rights, generally favouring the larger landowners in an area. Occasionally, enclosure occurred without hedges or walls, as in the Fens, though private fields here were usually defined by ditches.

The reasons for enclosure were complex and are still debated by historians. It certainly emerged out of the severe depopulation and economic shock of the Black Death, when livestock farming became more profitable. By the 18th century, it was being justified primarily in terms of agricultural improvement linked to Britain's Agricultural Revolution. However, some modern scholars have challenged the latter concept and the role of enclosure in boosting output. For others, it was essentially the legalised theft of land and a removal of rights that benefited the rich and condemned many commoners to poverty, enforced urbanisation or emigration.

In terms of removing Lincolnshire's open fields and commons, enclosure was not a quick process. It spanned 500 years from c. 1350 to c. 1850, during which time its impacts on the landscape evolved and changed. Broadly, enclosures which took place before c. 1650 are termed 'early', while those after c. 1700 increasingly involved an Act of Parliament – initially private, then public from 1801 – and are thus termed Parliamentary enclosures.

Early enclosure: plague, riots and the shift to grass

The 14th century was perhaps the most traumatic in England's recorded history, commencing with poor harvests and famine, then subject to the repeated episodes of plague from 1348-9. By 1400, England's population had been reduced by almost half and many villages had shrunk or disappeared altogether, especially in the Central Region noted previously. In this context, the feudal ties that had sustained the manorial system were fatally weakened. Landowners saw greater profits in pastoral farming and large areas of open fields were grassed over as sheepwalks, sometimes including villages. Peasants increasingly broke free from bonded labour and moved around more, some rising to become larger landowners in the new, more market-based economy. Conversely, others were reduced to dire poverty as access to their homes and livelihoods was removed. Social divisions were also exacerbated by emparkment (see Chapter 9).

Early enclosure caused political controversy and even insurrection, especially in the Midlands. In 1607, the Midland Revolt saw peasant riots and the uprooting of hedges on newly enclosed land in Northamptonshire, Leicestershire and Warwickshire. In Lincolnshire, opposition was focused

FACING PAGE: **former open fields at Frieston, Caythorpe, Kesteven.**
The open fields of Caythorpe underwent enclosure in 1657 by private Act of Parliament, though Caythorpe Heath remained as a common until 1762. The presence of isolated oaks in this sheep pasture may indicate a former hedgeline, or the area may once have been parkland for Frieston Old Hall. Ridge and furrow markings are still visible here as relict earthworks.

on the drainage of wetland commons, though the issue was essentially the same – hardship caused by loss of common grazing and other resources.

By the mid 16th century, population and cereal prices were recovering nationally, but the move to grass was entrenched, especially on clay soils. In Lincolnshire, the vales, Kesteven Uplands and coastal siltlands saw many parishes fully or partly enclosed. Essentially, grass then persisted in these areas until the second half of the 20th century, though the silt Fens are an exception, converting to arable in the 1800s. By contrast, cereals remained a key element in the light, 'sheep-corn' areas of the Wolds and Heath, which nevertheless retained extensive grazing on the upland commons until the Parliamentary phase of enclosure. Thus, in Tudor and Stuart times, Lincolnshire possessed distinct, specialised farming regions, each with

107

Parishes which underwent early enclosure are found throughout Lincolnshire, with notable concentrations in the vales and Kesteven Uplands (*Bennett & Bennett, 2001). Clearly, the hedged fields in such parishes mostly predate the Parliamentary phase of c. 1750 - c. 1850. However, care is needed when dating individual fields and hedges, as early enclosures were sometimes subdivided at a later date. Shrub diversity can be a useful indicator of a hedge's age, but most hedgerow trees are less than 250 years old, as replanting was normal from Medieval times until the early 1800s (Williamson, 2017). Ancient trees are mostly found in country house parks and areas used historically for hunting by the elite (see next chapter).

Early enclosed fields at **Edenham** (FACING PAGE) and **Newton-by-Toft** (RIGHT)

TOP RIGHT: **Bassingthorpe Manor.** A Tudor house built in 1568 with wool profits.

different landscape and field patterns (*Thirsk, 1957). To some extent these can still be traced today, albeit modified by later landscape changes.

Early enclosure varied in its field patterns, initially producing vast sheepwalks in some parishes, but later shifting to smaller, more regular fields as early closes were subdivided and further parishes enclosed. From the 16th to late 18th centuries, timber and wood were important for construction, shipbuilding and fuel, and hedgerows of this period were typically planted with trees for timber and/or pollarding, mostly oak or ash. In some parts of England, piecemeal enclosure created hedges that followed the reverse s-shaped form of the Medieval 'lands' and furlongs, though this appears uncommon in Lincolnshire, where larger-scale enclosure by agreement or landowner imposition was usual.

Hedges planted during the Parliamentary enclosures were initially like their predecessors, with trees planted at intervals to provide timber, fuelwood and aesthetic qualities. In Lincolnshire, ash and oak remained the most commonly used species, with beech on the uplands after c. 1750. In the 1800s, however, the railways made coal widely available in rural areas, rendering wood less important, while landowners increasingly saw plantation woodland as the appropriate location for timber production. Consequently, later Parliamentary hedges typically lacked trees and were usually of a single shrub species, usually hawthorn. Dating hedges requires care, however, as some species including ash can become established as trees by self-seeding. Conversely, many hedgerow trees were removed by farmers during the Agricultural Revolution and subsequently.

LEFT: **beech trees in Parliamentary hedgeline of c. 1796, Dunston Heath**

FACING PAGE: **late Parliamentary enclosure hedge, Hemingby, Wolds**

Parliamentary enclosure: the surveyor's rule and the end of the commons

The Parliamentary enclosures were arguably the most abrupt remodelling of the rural landscape in Lincolnshire's history. Over a period of less than one hundred years – from c. 1760 to c. 1850 – they removed all the remaining open fields outside of the Isle of Axholme, and also saw the reclamation and enclosure of virtually all surviving rough commons in the uplands and wetlands. Of the latter, only the peat bog at Crowle Moor and the turbary commons in Axholme survived. Early enclosure had affected perhaps half of all Lincolnshire's parishes already, but the twin onslaught of the Parliamentary phase nevertheless transformed the countryside. Appointed commissioners and surveyors usually replanned the parish in question, allotting all the remaining unenclosed land as private

The Lincoln Heath is probably the best example in Lincolnshire of upland common enclosed in the Parliamentary phase. The high plateau underwent conversion to farmland from unenclosed 'heath' in the period c. 1760 - c. 1800, having previously been used for centuries for common grazing and warrening by the villages on its periphery. The open, gorsy grasslands were enclosed to form private fields that were used mainly for mixed 'corn and sheep' farming, though commercial warrening continued into the 1820s around Temple Bruer (Mills, undated). The new fields were enclosed by drystone walls or hawthorn hedges, most of which are still present. Sadly, many of the walls are decaying as the shift to cash cropping since 1945 has reduced the need for stockproof barriers. The 'heaths' of the Wolds underwent a similar enclosure, though it took longer to complete and walls were rarely used.

LEFT: **limestone wall detail, Scopwick Heath**

BOTTOM LEFT: **farmstead of Parliamentary era, Normanton Heath**

FACING PAGE: **stormclouds over Canwick Heath**

fields and adding new, straight roads of a standard width. The extensive 'heath' commons of the Lincoln Heath and Wolds disappeared under the plough, as did all the remaining Fen wetlands. Agriculturally, it was certainly an audacious and remarkable undertaking that greatly increased Lincolnshire's arable acreage (though the contribution from ploughing up the old Fenland pastures should not be forgotten). It was also undeniably a key underpinning for industrial 'high farming' to develop in the 19th century, encouraging estates and tenant farmers to invest in improving their livestock, crop husbandry and farmsteads. Socially, however, there was a harsh corollary, as not all former smallholders or commoners gained a new

livelihood in farm labour or lived in the new model cottages provided by 'improving' landlords. Ecologically, too, reclamation caused massive loss of habitats and species, especially in the wetlands, even if extra hedges may have benefited woodland birds in former open-field areas (Williamson, 2002).

\-

The physical legacy of enclosure still defines most of the Lincolnshire countryside today despite later changes. Many hedgerows were lost in the decades after World War II as agricultural subsidies and larger farm machinery led to field amalgamation. However, a more conservation-based approach has dramatically slowed removal in recent decades, and hedgerows of different historical phases still survive widely. Replanting has occurred in places and traditional hedgelaying has also seen a revival in Lincolnshire in recent years. Perhaps the greatest concern today is for the future of ash as a hedgerow tree, with heavy losses expected from ash dieback fungus (*Chalara fraxinea*) over the coming decades. The future of Lincolnshire's drystone walls is also uncertain, though happily some farmers have been rebuilding with the help of subsidies since the 1980s.

112

TOP LEFT: **ivy and hawthorn berries in hedge near Folkingham, Kesteven**

LEFT: **recently layed hedge, Roxholm, Lincoln Heath.** Traditional hedgerow management varied according to individual landlord and land use, with areas of livestock farming and/or organised fox hunting typically having more frequent laying to produce a lower and tighter hedgerow.

References

Beastall, T.W. (1978), *The Agricultural Revolution in Lincolnshire*, Society for Lincolnshire History & Archaeology

Fulton, T. (2011), *A Treasure Beneath Our Feet: The Fields of Belton in Axholme*, Birkrigg Books

Mills, D.R. (1959), *Enclosure in Kesteven*, The Agricultural History Review, Vol. 7, No. 2, 1959

Mills, D.R. (undated leaflet), *The Heath Trail: A Country Drive*, North Kesteven District Council

Russell, E. & Russell, R.C. (1987), *Parliamentary Enclosure & New Lincolnshire Landscapes*, Lincolnshire County Council

Williamson, T. (2002), *Hedges and Walls*, The National Trust

Williamson, T. et al (2017), *Trees in England: Management and disease since 1600*, University of Hertfordshire Press

RIGHT: **hedgerow with ash tree, Stainton-by-Langworth, Lindsey Vale**

8 : PATHS, BRIDLEWAYS, TRACKS & LANES
Local Routes in the Countryside

We saw in Chapter 4 how a network of trackways and pathways had emerged in Lincolnshire by the Iron Age, some parts of which may date back to the Bronze Age and possibly even earlier. The impact of the Roman occupation on this prehistoric network has also been considered in Chapter 5. This chapter now looks at the network of *local* routes that survives in the countryside today, focusing on features that originated mainly for movement within parishes and between nearby settlements from Medieval times onwards. Chapter 14 picks up the story of longer distance routes, including the development of turnpike roads and drovers' ways.

Definitions: highways, byways & green lanes

Defining the terms 'path', 'track' and 'lane' can be a confusing business. 'Path' and 'bridleway' clearly imply foot and horse traffic respectively, but 'track' and 'lane' are applied to a variety of routes ranging from footpaths to metalled roads. The access rights relating to routes add further terms

and complexity, but are perhaps a good place to start. Basically, there is a legal distinction between highways – routes on which the public has a right of access – and private ways, where access rights are restricted to named individuals. Highways include public footpaths, public bridleways and byways – collectively known as public rights of way – as well as public roads, each category having its own use rights. Motorised vehicles cannot

115

FACING PAGE: **bridleway near Thoresway, Lincolnshire Wolds**

RIGHT: **green lane near Kelby, Kesteven Uplands**

legally use public footpaths or bridleways, though some byways can be so used despite most being unsurfaced. Thus, a Byway Open to All Traffic (BOAT) is open to motorised vehicles while a Restricted Byway (RB) is not. Most byways in Lincolnshire are restricted, but the question of motor traffic using unsurfaced tracks is complicated by another category of public road called an unsurfaced, unclassified county road (UCR), to which legal access by motor vehicle has been established in most cases (LCC, 2014).

'Green lane' obviously has greater appeal for most people than these technical terms, though it confers no legal status by itself. It does, however, have an official definition, being 'an unmetalled path or track bounded by hedges, walls or ditches' (Belsey, 2001). It can be applied to routes from any period of history and encompasses paths, bridleways, byways and drovers' ways, some of which form part of longer distance routes.

Not all paths, tracks or green lanes have a public right of way, so users are advised to check on maps beforehand. Conversely, rights of way have been augmented recently by Permissive Paths, where the landowner has agreed to public access. These routes are usually shown by signage at the location.

So much for definitions and legalities. It is now time to consider the historical legacy of local routes in the countryside. 'Path' and 'lane' are used here in a non-legal sense to mean foot and carriage routes respectively, while present-day unsurfaced routes are termed 'green lanes' or 'tracks' as best fits.

LEFT: **Lenton's Lane, Friskney Tofts, Fens**

The Medieval legacy: what has survived the enclosures?

The history of local access routes in Lincolnshire is closely linked to the progress of enclosure (see Chapter 7). While there were undoubtedly paths and tracks giving access to industrial sites such as quarries and for other purposes, Medieval Lincolnshire away from the coastline was essentially agricultural. Local routes within the parish were therefore primarily for moving people, livestock and produce between the village, its open fields and other lands (meadow, pasture, woods and wild commons). The inhabitants of a Medieval parish or 'vill' would have had access to most of the land within it, and a dense network of tracks and paths would have existed. Travel to adjoining settlements was also important during the Medieval period, including visits to markets and fairs in nearby towns.

So, does anything survive of this Medieval local network? As we saw with fields, much depends on the timing and nature of the enclosure process at the individual parish level. Broadly, parishes which experienced significant enclosure before the Parliamentary phase of c. 1760 - c. 1850 are more likely to have retained Medieval routes, even if these have changed in

The Isle of Axholme has more pre-enclosure landscape than other parts of Lincolnshire due to the retention of its open fields. The relict open field areas surrounding the Isle's villages are crossed by many footpaths and tracks which almost certainly originated in the Medieval or early post-Medieval period. These examples are at **Low Burnham** (TOP RIGHT) and **Haxey** (RIGHT). Tracks between the villages and their turbaries are thought to date back at least to the reclamation and enclosure of the Axholme wetlands in the 1600s.

Proving that a particular lane, track or path existed prior to enclosure, let alone in Medieval times, can be difficult and is not always possible based on the historical evidence and archaeology currently available. However, the name and form of a route may offer circumstantial evidence for a pre-enclosure origin. Thus, lane names referring to former open fields (e.g. south field, west field, etc) or to furlongs strongly suggest a pre-enclosure and possibly Medieval origin. Similarly, names including 'moor', 'heath', 'fen' or 'carr' may indicate that the route predates the reclamation and enclosure of the parish's rough commons (though this requires care as these often survived after the open fields were enclosed). Narrow and/or sunken lanes are another indicator of routes older than Parliamentary enclosure. The following examples of probable pre-enclosure routes are all in parishes enclosed privately before the Parliamentary phase.

LEFT: **Somerby Wold Lane, Somerby, Wolds**

BOTTOM LEFT: **Dike Furlong Lane, Hough-on-the-Hill, Kesteven**

FACING PAGE: **Narrow Moor Lane, Bassingham, Vale of Trent**

purpose and/or legal status over time. Thus, it is often possible here to find lanes, tracks or paths which maintain the alignment, physical boundaries and even hedges of pre-enclosure routes. The old village core is a good place to start when looking for these, as the tracks that gave access to the open fields converged here and can survive as modern lanes or farm tracks. Sunken lanes in particular are indicative of long use and a probable Medieval or even earlier origin. Sometimes it is possible to trace how

surviving routes related to the open fields and/or other elements of the pre-enclosure parish, such as woods or commons. Routes leading from a village to its former heath, moor or wetland are also worth investigating.

As with fields, there is marked regional variation in the pattern of surviving routes in the different landscape character areas of Lincolnshire. Medieval lanes and 'droves' occur frequently around the Wash in the Townlands and their reclaimed wetlands, and also in the Lindsey Outmarsh. In the wider Fens, fen banks and the embankments of rivers and drains also provided routes for travel from Medieval times onwards. The Isle of Axholme is unique within Lincolnshire in that its open fields avoided enclosure; even today it retains early paths and tracks in the landscape to an unusual degree. By contrast, most parish lanes on the upland 'heaths' and Wolds were laid out in their current form during the Parliamentary enclosures, though some were probably older in origin (see caption below).

Many new roads were laid out when Lincolnshire's upland commons or 'heaths' were reclaimed as farmland during the Parliamentary enclosures. The Lincoln Heath, Lincoln Cliff and Wolds still have some of the best examples of these Parliamentary era landscapes. However, the uplands were not trackless before enclosure, and still retain various older routes with prehistoric, Roman and Medieval origins. As well as long-distance roads, local routes developed for moving livestock between settlements and their upland grazing land. Additionally, the Lincoln Heath retains routes that were probably established by the Knights Templar for travel and transport of wool and other produce from their farming estates at Temple Bruer and East Mere (Mills, 2009).

FACING PAGE: **valley route to Caistor High Street, Wolds**

RIGHT: **green lane near Temple Bruer.** A Knights Templar trackway?

The Parliamentary enclosures: new roads for new landscapes?

The situation for parishes that underwent enclosure wholly or mainly by Act of Parliament is theoretically very different, in that the appointed surveyors often refashioned the internal layout of the parish (or part of the parish) concerned, including its local roads. Typically, broad new roads of a specified width were laid out on straight courses, along with private roads giving access to the new farms located away from the village.

However, evidence suggests that the redrawing of local route networks by Parliamentary enclosure was not always as total as some historians have suggested (Russell & Russell, 1987). The persistence of prehistoric and Roman roads is explored elsewhere, but even local routes could survive. The Parliamentary commissioners had the power to confirm existing routes for public or private use as well as to create new ones (Breen, 2017). In some cases, existing routes were simply upgraded by straightening or widening, with the addition of new hedges. So, even in these parishes, paths, tracks and lanes potentially predate enclosure and may originate in the Medieval period or earlier. Unfortunately, few parishes were

Roads created or upgraded during Parliamentary enclosure are relatively wide and were usually defined by new hawthorn hedges or (on the Lincoln Heath) drystone walls. Trees were planted in these boundaries for fuel and aesthetic reasons until roughly the second quarter of the 19th century, when coal became increasingly available in the countryside. These scenes on Parliamentary enclosure roads are at **Thoresway, Wolds** (LEFT) and **Green Man Lane, Lincoln Heath** (FACING PAGE).

122

The origin of paths and lanes can sometimes be inferred from historical records of enclosure, including Parliamentary enclosure awards. Caution is needed, however, as the enclosure process and its relationship to such routes can be complex and unexpected.

FACING PAGE: **footpath between Fotherby and North Elkington, Wolds.** Fotherby was enclosed by Act of Parliament of 1764, yet this public footpath appears to be part of an older route to the deserted Medieval village of North Elkington in the adjoining parish.

RIGHT: **Warren Lane, Temple Bruer.** This green lane is bounded by stone walls and planted beech trees that almost certainly date to Parliamentary enclosure. However, Mills (2009) suggests this route was the predecessor of Bishop Alnwick's 16th century 'broad strete'.

BOTTOM RIGHT: **lane near Cumberworth, Lindsey Marsh.** Cumberworth underwent Parliamentary enclosure in the 1820s, but almost half the parish had already been enclosed privately before that date (Russell & Russell, 1987). This lane passes through an area of old enclosures and could therefore be Medieval in origin.

mapped in detail prior to their Parliamentary enclosure awards, such that proving the existence of older routes can be difficult. Nevertheless, footpaths connecting adjacent villages are particularly worth investigation, while a path which stops abruptly at a parish boundary may also indicate the partial survival of an earlier route.

Most public roads laid out in the Parliamentary enclosures survive today as surfaced lanes, usually with wide grassy verges either side of a tarmacked

carriageway. Originally, they would have been unsurfaced, and some still are, remaining as green lanes or field tracks. Superficially, these can appear similar to – and in some cases may actually be – older, pre-enclosure routes, but they usually retain the broad dimensions specified in the relevant Parliamentary enclosure award.

Lincolnshire's network of local routes has continued to evolve since the completion of the Parliamentary enclosures in the mid 19th century, reflecting wider changes in farming and the countryside over the last two centuries. However, despite losses and damage to public footpaths from ploughing, the county still possesses a rich legacy of local routes including many of Medieval origin. These offer great opportunities for further historical research, as we have only scratched the surface in our understanding in many cases. And, whatever their histories, Lincolnshire's paths, bridleways, tracks and lanes remain by far the best way to explore the countryside, as well as providing an important linear network of habitats for wildlife and nature conservation.

TOP LEFT: **sloes in hedgerow, King Steet, Kesteven**

LEFT: **wild flowers on verge, Bloxholm Lane, Lincoln Heath.** Path margins and road verges are an important wildlife habitat in Lincolnshire, often retaining species that have disappeared from agricultural land. Verge flora reflect the local geology and soils of each area, such as the limestone grassland seen here.

References

Belsey, V. (2001), *Discovering Green Lanes*, Green Book, Totnes, Devon

Breen, T. (2017), *Public or Private? An Analysis of the Legal Status of Rights of Way in Norfolk*, in Landscapes, Vol. 18, No. 1, June 2017, Routledge

Hindle, P. (1998), *Medieval Roads and Tracks*, Shire Publications

Lincolnshire County Council (2014), *Draft Lincolnshire Rights of Way Improvement Plan, 2014 - 2019*

Mills, D. (revised 2009), *The Knights Templar in Kesteven*, Heritage Lincolnshire

Russell, E. & Russell, R.C. (1985), *Old & New Landscapes in the Horncastle Area*, Lincolnshire County Council

Russell, E. & Russell, R.C. (1987), *Parliamentary Enclosure & New Lincolnshire Landscapes*, Lincolnshire County Council

RIGHT: **public bridleway, Haxey Turbary, Isle of Axholme**

9 : PARKS & PLANTATIONS
Aristocratic Lines in the Landscape

The role of elites in defining the landscape has a long pedigree in Britain, extending back at least as far back as the Bronze Age. At Stonehenge (Wilts), individuals with material wealth and influence ensured that their round barrows were constructed in prime locations overlooking the Neolithic stone circle, thereby creating an elite monumental landscape. Later, the Romans, and their client elites imposed villa estates on parts the farmed countryside of south-east Britain, presumably usurping farmland in the process. It is with the Norman Conquest, however, that elite power and the ownership of land really starts to dominate the appearance of the countryside.

This chapter explores how the landowning class has added its own set of linear features as it moulded Lincolnshire's landscape from Medieval times, focusing particularly on the evolving aesthetic tastes and sporting pursuits of the aristocracy and gentry. Today, the physical legacy remains strong and visible, manifested most obviously in the historic parks and gardens of country houses and even more widely, if perhaps less appreciated, in the wider landscaping of landed estates, including plantation woodlands, fox coverts and even hedgerows and their trees.

FACING PAGE: **beech avenue, Burton Hall estate, Lincoln Cliff**

RIGHT: **old lime pollard with mistletoe, Grimsthorpe Park, Kesteven**

Medieval hunting landscapes: forests and deer parks

There had been land used primarily for hunting by the monarch and the aristocracy in Anglo-Saxon England, but it was the Norman Conquest which began the setting aside of large areas of countryside for hunting, principally of deer, by the monarch and nobles. These were known as 'forests' and 'chases' respectively and typically encompassed a range of habitats including heath and fen as well as woodland. The land within

forests and chases was managed to promote better hunting, but was defined more by its legal status than by physical boundary features. In particular, Forest Law was applied in the royal hunting forests, modified by the Charter of the Forest in 1217 to give freemen greater rights of access.

Generally much smaller and physically bounded by a ditched bank and 'pale' were deer parks, belonging to manorial lords or other wealthy individuals. They were primarily for the farming of deer to provide venison, and were apparently rarely used for hunting deer. Deer parks reached their heyday in the 13th and early 14th centuries, when most were remote from the landowner's dwelling. However, some Medieval deer parks were 'country house' parks, especially after c. 1350, forming the setting for the dwellings of the upper class. A grand park typically included lawns, ornamental tree planting, fishponds, orchard, kitchen garden and a pleasure garden or 'herber' (Uglow, 2004). The 'herber' was an enclosed, private garden bounded by walls, hedges or trellis – a place of Medieval romance and eroticism.

Medieval deer parks declined after c. 1300 and most disappeared through landscape change, either being converted to farmland or incorporated into landscape parkland as more country houses became established in the countryside from Tudor times. Survivals in the modern landscape are therefore rare and often poorly documented.

130

TOP LEFT: **former Forest of Kesteven, Grimsthorpe Park**

LEFT: **Lion Gate, Scrivelsby Park**

Tudor and Early Stuart parks: the growth of country houses and emparkment

In Tudor and Stuart times, parks became more numerous and more sophisticated as individual expressions of elite taste, with the styles of France, Italy and the Netherlands providing aspirational models for the wealthy and powerful. The formal garden remained as a key element within the estate of the Tudor country house, but became more elaborate and theatrical with the addition of viewing mounds, terraces, gazebos, mazes, canals and fountains. The Tudor 'knot garden' gave way in the early 17th century to formal *parterres* following Continental styles. Elite gardens in Stuart times reflected contemporary interests in science and metaphysics,

with fantastical grottos and use of symbolism. Beyond the formal garden lay the park, which continued to evolve though had yet to undergo the design revolutions of the late 17th and 18th centuries (see next section). The growth of country houses and their parks established an ongoing and controversial association between emparkment and enclosure. Put simply, a landowner

ABOVE: **Aswarby Park.** Aswarby was the seat of the Carre family in Tudor times. The park may date back to the 1600s and clearly shows ridge and furrow markings, suggesting it was created wholly or partly by the emparkment of open fields. The Medieval village of Aswarby was moved when the park was expanded in the 19th century. The house was demolished in 1951, though its position is still marked by the two Georgian columns visible on the left of the picture.

who wanted to create or extend a park would often simply convert tenants' fields or common land, sometimes relocating or removing a village in the process. Such parks can, however, offer valuable insights into the Tudor countryside, as they effectively 'fossilised' elements of the pre-existing landscape. In particular, ancient trees were usually retained to give the park a suitably established feel (Rackham, 2004).

Revolutions in the park, c. 1660 - c. 1770: André Le Nôtre to Lancelot 'Capability' Brown

The restoration of the monarchy in 1660 marked the beginning of a revolutionary period in park design, leading ultimately to the English Landscape Style popularised by 'Capability' Brown and his followers from the 1750s. Change started after the Civil War with the importation by Charles II and others of the French garden style perfected at Versailles by

FACING PAGE: **Belton Park.** Belton Park is a notable example of landscape parkland of the late 1600s. Its design has formal avenues within a grand landscape scheme which utilises the topography of the Lincoln Edge and views to the surrounding countryside. Belmount Tower is a later addition of c. 1750.

TOP RIGHT: **Culverthorpe Hall, Kesteven.** The pitched roof and central chimneys of the hall are thought to date to c. 1679, predating the alterations of the 18th century. This view through limes evokes the Continental formality of Restoration era parkland.

RIGHT: **Belton House.** This neoclassical house dates from c. 1685 and is widely regarded as the finest surviving country house of this period in England.

Grimsthorpe Park is thought to date to the mid 1600s, and is perhaps the grandest and best-preserved park of this period in Britain. Many of the surviving avenues and 'rides' of oaks were probably planted at this time, though like other early parks it incorporated older elements from the pre-existing countryside, including oak trees from Medieval hedgerows and wood pasture (Rackham, 2004). The park underwent successive changes over the centuries, producing the complex palimpsest seen today. The remodelling of the Castle with a neo-classical north front in c. 1685 was accompanied by the establishment of the main axial avenue. The latter was then remodelled in c. 1711 by the creation of a Dutch-style 'bastion garden' by Stephen Switzer, who also introduced the concept of 'naturalistic' vistas linking to the surrounding countryside. Parts of the park were then reworked by 'Capability' Brown from the 1740s with drainage engineer John Grundy.

FACING PAGE: **oak-lined ride, probably mid 17ᵗʰ century**

RIGHT & BOTTOM RIGHT: **main axial avenue of c. 1685**

135

André Le Nôtre (1613 - 1700) – chief garden designer for Louis XIV – with its vistas, avenues, strict formality and infinite distances. Under this influence, parks became grand designs, usually with a main axial avenue and starbursts of secondary avenues radiating from nodes. Examples can still be seen at Belton Park and Grimsthorpe Park, both of which retain avenues and rides dating to the 1680s, despite later changes. By the early 1700s, however, there were calls for a more naturalistic, specifically English style of landscape gardening. Historians of the subject have long debated exactly how and when this occurred, as well as which parks and designers were key, but there is clearly an initial phase of 'softening' of formality

Like many of Lincolnshire's country house parks, **Brocklesby Park** (LEFT) has undergone successive revisions and additions dating back to Tudor times. However, the core of landscaped parkland stretching between **Newsham Lake** (FACING PAGE) and Great Limber village is essentially the work of Lancelot 'Capabilty' Brown, who was commissioned in 1771 to make alterations to the house and park. Characteristically, Brown's scheme was bounded by an informal belt of plantation woodland using mixed hardwoods. The park was greatly extended south of Great Limber with landscaping by Thomas White in the late 1700s and further modifications, probably additional lakes, were made by Humphry Repton. Extensive tree planting continued on the estate into the 19th century, and Pelham's Pillar was erected in the 1840s to commemorate the Earl of Yarborough's addition of several million trees. Today, large areas of former park are arable but much of Brown's core survives. The park is privately owned and accessible only via public highways and a number of permissive trails that are open seasonally.

after c. 1710. This is usually attributed to Stephen Switzer (1682 - 1745) who, despite retaining formal garden elements in his schemes, nevertheless opened out landscape parkland to connect visually with the surrounding countryside in a more naturalistic way, as at Grimsthorpe Park. This phase was followed from c. 1735 by a classical, allegorical style epitomised by William Kent (c. 1685 - 1748) and his park at Stowe (Bucks). Lastly, from the 1750s, came the radical, 'naturalistic' parkland of Lancelot 'Capability' Brown (c. 1715 - 1783) and his followers, which completely eschewed Continental formality in favour of informal woodland blocks and clumps, scattered trees and serpentine lakes. Typically, parkland now swept right up to the house itself, interrupted only by a ha-ha of brick or stone. Lincolnshire has several parks on which Brown worked, including Brocklesby, Grimsthorpe and Hainton, with further important examples nearby at Belvoir Castle (Leics / Lincs) and Burghley (Cambs).

The age of 'improvement', c. 1700 - c. 1920: patriotism, progress and plantations

By the late 18th century and the end of 'Capability' Brown's life, his style of parkland was becoming unfashionable with the rise of Romantic aesthetics and Picturesque taste in landscape, though Humphry Repton (1752 - 1818) initially followed some of Brown's ideas with modifications. Repton's principal work in Lincolnshire is Scrivelsby Park, dating to before 1791 (*Pevsner, 1989). However, Lincolnshire's relatively subdued terrain did not lend itself easily to Romantic landscaping as popularised by John Ruskin and others, and more conservative parkland design elements such as avenues and clumps often continued here through the 19th century.

Perhaps of greater overall significance to the landscape than this national stylistic debate was the widespread commitment amongst the 18th and 19th century aristocracy to the idea of 'improvement'. This reflected the prevailing 'patriotic' view of Britain as a uniquely liberal, progressive and scientific nation, contrasted at the time with Continental absolutism

A landscape plan for the Belvoir estate (Leics / Lincs) was prepared by 'Capability' Brown shortly before his death in 1783. Implementation was partly posthumous and, unlike his earlier schemes, retained adjoining villages including **Woolsthorpe** (FACING PAGE), as well as existing formal garden and terrace elements, thus reflecting the emerging 'medievalist' taste of the Regency era (Duchess of Rutland & Pruden, 2015).

RIGHT: **Belvoir Castle (Leics)**. The castle itself was rebuilt between 1801 and 1830 in Gothic Revival style, dominating its estate and the surrounding countryside.

139

140

and decadence. Increasingly, landowners were expected to manage their estates in a correspondingly patriotic and efficient manner. In parallel with the Agricultural Revolution and the consequent development of Victorian high farming, many estates underwent extensive tree planting, with new plantation woodlands producing timber using 'scientific forestry' rather than traditional woodmanship (Williams, 2013). Planting was often applied across entire estates, providing appropriately naturalistic landscaping as well as cover for game birds. Some parts of Lincolnshire also saw the creation of coverts to encourage foxes for local hunts, though less so than in neighbouring Leicestershire and Rutland (Finch, 2004).

Initially, plantation woodland used mainly oak, due to its patriotic associations and the demand from shipbuilding, especially for the navy. In the 19th century, other tree species became more common, including softwoods. As in previous centuries, the creation of parkland often involved the enclosure of open fields or rough commons. This is well seen on the Brocklesby Estate in Lincolnshire, where woods were planted across a vast area of land enclosed from the northern Wolds in the early 19th century.

The 20th century saw many country houses demolished or converted to new uses. Nevertheless, they and their estates remain as a defining legacy in the landscape across much of Lincolnshire today.

TOP LEFT: **estate farmland with plantation woodlands, Croxby, Wolds**

LEFT: **woodland blocks in farmed landscape, Walcot, Kesteven Uplands**

References

Duchess of Rutland with Pruden, J. (2015), *Capability Brown & Belvoir: Discovering a Lost Landscape*, Nick McCann Associates

Finch, J. (2004), *'Grass, Grass, Grass': Fox-hunting and the Creation of the Modern Landscape*, in Landscapes, Volume 5, Number 2, Windgather Press

Manning, C.J. (2006), *Deer & Deer Parks of Lincolnshire*, Lincolnshire Naturalists' Union

Rackham, O. (2004), *Pre-Existing Trees & Woods in Country-House Parks*, in Landscapes, Volume 5, Number 2, Windgather Press

Sheeran, G. (2006), *Patriotic Views: Aristocratic Ideology and the Eighteenth-Century Landscape*, in Landscapes, Volume 7, Number 2, Windgather Press

Uglow, J. (2004), *A Little History of British Gardening*, Chatto & Windus

Williams, H. (2013), *Beauty and Profit: The Creation, Management and Harvesting of East Riding Estate Woodlands, 1750 - 1930*, in Landscapes, Volume 13, Number 2, Windgather Press

RIGHT: **model farm buildings of c. 1820, Scopwick.** This impressive complex of farm buildings was built by Henry Chaplin of the Blankney Estate. As progressive landlords, the Chaplins also constructed model cottages in Blankney village in the 1830s and 40s.

10 : SEA BANKS
Coastal Defence & Reclamation

The modern coastline of Lincolnshire is almost entirely low-lying and lacking in natural cliffs, making it vulnerable to tidal surges and flooding from the sea. Protection is provided today, as it has been since early Medieval times, by a combination of natural dunes (sometimes augmented by concrete sea defences) and man-made embankments along the high tide line of the saltmarshes and estuaries.

This chapter looks at sea banks in the Lincolnshire landscape from Anglo-Danish times to the present. The main focus is on the Wash, where their use has been particularly significant in the reclamation of tidal marshland to create new land for settlement and farming, and has left a succession of banks stranded in the modern farmscape. It should be remembered, however, that sea banks were also used for reclamation on parts of the North Sea coast, notably between Saltfleet and Grimsby, and along the Humber Bank. There was possibly also a Medieval sea bank in places between Skegness and Theddlethorpe before this stretch of coast lost land to the sea in Tudor times, and the present 'Roman Bank' or Commissioners Bank was built as a replacement (Robinson, 2001).

The inner margin of the Wash is today defined by its sea bank, running continuously from near Gibraltar Point to the chalk cliffs of Hunstanton in Norfolk. The only significant breaks occur at the Fenland rivers and their historic estuary ports, where sluices and flood defences of brick, concrete and steel take over. The modern sea bank both delineates and contains the highest tides around the Wash, and in a sense therefore constitutes the coastline. However, as the map on page 154 shows, it is only the youngest of several sea banks built around the Wash over the last 1,200 years.

143

FACING PAGE: **modern sea bank, Frampton Marsh**

RIGHT: **Peter Seadike Lane, Gosberton / Surfleet**

Early sea banks around the Wash

The story of coastal embanking around the Wash is thought to begin in the Anglo-Danish period, following the 'nucleation' that produced the 'primary' or 'parent' settlements of the Townlands. These fixed villages emerged following a seaward shift away from earlier locations in the face of advancing fen wetlands. They occupied the silt ridge fringing the then coastline of the Wash, which was penetrated by estuaries of varying size. Most settlements appear to have developed in sheltered locations by estuaries or creeks, which served as 'havens' for fishing and coastal trade.

As pioneer communities in a largely untamed coastal landscape, the villages began to develop and protect their field systems through embanking both seawards and inland in the fens (see next chapter). The first proper sea banks were almost certainly built by individual villages for their own protection, along tidal creeks and near estuaries, and probably commenced in the 9th or 10th centuries. Tentatively, examples of early banks or 'dykes' have been identified at Surfleet (Peter Sea Dyke and Cunsdyke), Donington (Donington Eaudyke), Kirton (Seadyke and Skeldyke), Friskney (Friskney Eaudyke/Low Road) and elsewhere. In some cases, as at Donington, the early local defences were later incorporated into

TOP LEFT: **saltmarsh patterns, the Scalp, Fishtoft**

LEFT: **saltmarsh pool at dawn, the Wash**

FACING PAGE: **River Welland and its sea banks, Fosdyke**

144

longer sections of bank and ultimately became part of the continuous Medieval Sea Bank protecting the entire Wash coastline (see below). Other early banks were rendered secondary or redundant by Medieval reclamation as the Townlands expanded seawards over the next four centuries.

Once surrounded by banks, the estuaries were easy targets for reclamation, especially in a context of natural coastal retreat. Bicker and Wrangle Havens survived until the 1600s despite becoming silted, but most of the smaller estuaries had gone by 1300. Away from the estuaries too, early reclamation soon pushed the coastline outwards, commencing before the Domesday Survey (1086), sometimes involving a succession of coastlines prior to the Medieval Sea Bank. In places, waste silt from early Medieval salterns helped to consolidate and extend new coastlines, as seen in the Tofts between Wrangle and Wainfleet.

The siltlands around the Wash are marked by a string of 'primary' villages that emerged through settlement 'nucleation' adjacent to the tidal zone in the Anglo-Danish period and became the main centres for the area's Medieval expansion of farming and maritime trade. The silting of estuaries and seaward reclamation of land over several centuries typically left these original settlements ever further from the sea, such as **Long Sutton** (LEFT). Reclamation using earthen banks was often followed by the establishment of 'daughter' settlements along a new coastline, while several of the original villages developed into small market towns or ports. The Townlands area is still distinct among the landscapes of Lincolnshire's Fenland in having an 'organic' countryside of considerable historical depth and long-established character.

The countryside between the Townland settlements and the Medieval Sea Bank has a rich and fascinating landscape history. The area retains many features that have persisted since the earliest phases of embanking and land reclamation in the Anglo-Danish period. Early sea banks can often still be traced as lanes and pathways that wind around former estuaries long absorbed into the farmed landscape, as here at **Skeldyke near Kirton** (RIGHT). Early land reclamations are recorded by historical field names such as 'newland' and in surviving field boundaries and other landscape features. This lane at **Leverton** (BOTTOM RIGHT) marks the outermost of three former coastlines, all of probable pre-Domesday date, within the unitary Medieval Sea Bank of Leverton parish, here thought to be 12th century or later.

147

'Roman Bank' : a unitary Medieval sea bank?

At some point in the Townlands' Medieval expansion, it seems likely that a continuous 'unitary' sea bank was conceived for the Wash as a whole. Certainly by 1300 and possibly earlier, Medieval banks ran along the entire western and southern sides of the Wash, protecting the Townlands and the corresponding Norfolk Marshland. Most scholars consider Croft Bank, between Wainfleet and Skegness, to be of similar date (Robinson, 2001). Today, this outermost Medieval sea bank is still a remarkable feature in the landscape, with many stretches of well-preserved, earthen embankment. Modern Ordnance Survey maps formally designate it as *Sea Bank* in gothic

typeface, denoting an important historic monument. The prominence and apparent masterplanning of the bank attracted the attention of antiquarians too, who erroneously named it Roman Bank in the 17th century. Modern investigation has definitively shown the bank to be of Medieval origin.

Many questions still surround this earthwork, however, and particularly whether it can truly be regarded as a single, co-ordinated defence as is often claimed. Various suggestions have been put forward for the authority behind such a project, including the monasteries, an enlightened Anglo-Saxon thegn and, perhaps most feasibly, Danish administration related to the area's wapentakes. Firm evidence for early co-ordination is thin, though, and both the archaeological and historical records suggest the unitary Sea Bank is actually a composite work undertaken in different centuries, both pre- and post-1066, with some sections probably dating from as early as the 9th or 10th centuries and others probably as late as the 13th century. As a further complication, there was apparently separate political administration east and west of the Nene estuary, the ancient boundary between East Anglia

The Medieval Sea Bank is one of the most impressive earthworks in Lincolnshire, yet remains enigmatic. Now lying several miles inland of the sea, it is thought to mark the Wash coastline as it existed in c. 1300. Today, long stretches of the bank survive intact and can be followed as public footpaths and tracks, while other sections have lost height but are still traceable as routes or other features passing through the countryside and former coastal settlements. These scenes show the Medieval Sea Bank at **Saltergate, Friskney** (TOP LEFT), **Frampton** (LEFT) and **Leverton** (FACING PAGE).

and Middle Anglia, and later between Norfolk and Lincolnshire. The process by which the Medieval Sea Bank was planned as a continuous sea defence, if such it was, therefore seems likely to remain obscure. Indeed, it is entirely possible that the Sea Bank is simply a 'snapshot' in an ongoing process of Medieval coastal reclamation.

If the origins of the Medieval Sea Bank are still hazy, its overall significance for Holland and the Fens is nevertheless clear. While it did not eliminate the danger from flooding – many damaging storm surges and fatalities are recorded through Medieval times and after – the improved security enabled the Townlands to develop and expand into one of the most prosperous areas in England by the 13th century, with numerous fine churches reflecting its agricultural and trading wealth. It also facilitated Medieval expansion into the adjoining fens, as explored in the next chapter.

Post-Medieval reclamation: from Vermuyden to MAFF and beyond

After the Medieval Sea Bank, it was more than three hundred years before the next sea banks were constructed around the Wash. Coastal reclamation revived in the 1630s, with large-scale schemes occurring in the Nene estuary (1632) and from Wrangle to Wainfleet (c. 1641), followed by a colossal intake of over 17,000 acres between Moulton and Gedney undertaken by Vermuyden after the Civil War. The silted havens at Bicker and Wrangle were also reclaimed at this time. Despite later removal by landowners or farmers, sections of 17th century bank can

still be seen in places, as at Wrangle and Friskney. Here, the reclaimed marshland also retains in part its original field pattern of elongated enclosures which extended the earlier, Medieval plots created by saltmaker-farmers in the adjoining Tofts.

In the 18th and 19th centuries, marshland reclamation increasingly went hand in hand with enclosure (see Chapter 7). Activity focused on the south side of the Wash, where the South Holland Embankment Act lead to the creation of 4,695 acres of new land for farming between 1793 and 1811. As in the Medieval period, marshland reclamation was followed by the establishment of daughter settlements, including Gedney Drove End, Gedney Dawsmere, Holbeach St. Matthew and Holbeach St. Marks, which later became separate parishes. Other features of the landscape – drains, roads, farmsteads and woods – probably emerged through a mixture of informal evolution and planning. Land was generally left for a decade following reclamation before it became dry enough for ploughing and crops. Saltmarsh creeks were usually left initially before the imposition of straight, artificial drains, though some sections of the original drainage were retained and have survived until the present day.

The outermost bank – today's sea bank – is actually an amalgam of piecemeal reclamations rather than a single project, and contains sections completed in various decades from the 1830s to the 1970s. As late as 1983, the then Ministry of Agriculture, Fisheries and Food (MAFF) prepared a map showing areas of 'Green Marsh' with reclamation potential, the only constraints indicated being the MOD's bombing ranges and engineering difficulties. By the mid 1980s, however, a new social and environmental context had emerged of increasing ecological awareness, reduced state spending and rising sea levels, effectively bringing the long era of land reclamation in the Wash to an end. Plans to reclaim the entire bay, Dutch-style, have occasionally resurfaced, but the international importance of the Wash for wildlife is now uppermost in public policy.

In the 21st century, even the role of sea banks is being challenged and managed retreat is increasingly accepted as the best response to climate change and the loss of saltmarsh. Freiston Shore is an early example

Bicker Haven is the largest of the extinct estuaries around the Wash in Lincolnshire and has an intriguing history. It is thought to have been the principal estuary of the River Witham until the early 11th century, when floods caused the main river to divert to its present course further north. Bicker Haven remained as an estuary with a shipping trade, but gradually became silted and was reclaimed in the mid 1600s by sealing off its mouth. Salt making was important here from Anglo-Saxon times, producing large quantities of silt waste that can still be seen in the modern landscape as low hills. Medieval salt making was located on the seaward side of coastal defences to allow direct access to tidal brine, so reference to active salterns in documents such as the Domesday Book may therefore help in dating sections of sea bank. Thus, the Medieval Sea Bank was probably continous around Bicker Haven by 1086. Care is required, however, as Medieval saltern waste is not absent within the Sea Bank as has sometimes been claimed. Reclamation left the Sea Bank stranded inland, though it largely survived as a convenient causeway for lanes and paths. Today, some stretches are public rights of way, as here at **Sutterton Dowdyke** (FACING PAGE).

where the modern sea bank has been deliberately breached to create new saltmarsh to absorb storm surges and benefit wildlife. Within the sea bank too, the RSPB has created an important wetland habitat by rewetting farmland at Frampton Marsh. Here, it is possible to imagine the dynamic transition or 'ecotone' of natural habitats that once existed between the freshwater fens and coastal saltmarshes before embanking and, perhaps, a new future for Lincolnshire's coastal lowlands if sea level continues to rise as predicted.

FACING PAGE: **new saltmarsh, Freiston.** The outer sea bank on the horizon was completed in 1979 by prison inmates and staff of nearby HMP North Sea Camp. The reclamation was short-lived, however, as the wall was deliberately breached in 2000 to benefit wildlife and provide a buffer zone against storms as part of coastal managed retreat. The area is now part of the RSPB's Freiston Shore reserve along with the former borrow pit from which the clay for the sea banks was extracted.

TOP RIGHT: **ornithological artwork, Frampton Marsh RSPB reserve**

RIGHT: **1809 sea bank and 1970s reclaimed farmland, Benington Sea End**

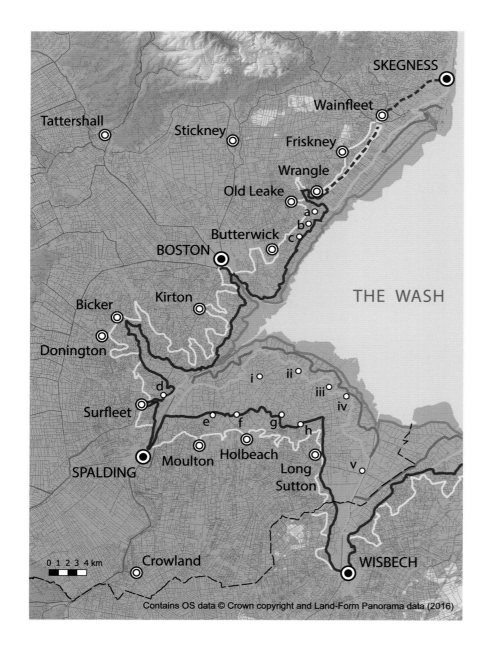

Sea Banks around the Wash in Lincolnshire

MEDIEVAL

— probable Anglo-Danish coastline , c. AD 900

— coastline of c. 1300 (= 'unitary' Medieval Sea Bank)

— the Tofts ridge (Wrangle to Wainfleet)

Coastal daughter settlements established by c. 1300:

a - *Leake Hurn's End*

b - *Leverton Lucasgate & Leverton Outgate*

c - *Benington Sea End*

d - *Surfleet Seas End*

e - *Moulton Seas End*

f - *Holbeach Clough & Holbeach Bank*

g - *Holbeach Hurn*

h - *Gedney Dyke*

POST-MEDIEVAL

Outer limit of reclamation by sea banks by date:

— 1700

— 1800

— 1983

Post-Medieval settlements on reclaimed coastal land:

i - *Holbech St. Marks*

ii - *Holbeach St. Matthew*

iii - *Dawsmere*

iv - *Gedney Drove End*

v - *Sutton Bridge*

Source: MAFF (1983) with additional information from Hallam (1965)

References

Cope-Faulkner, P. et al (2010), *Wide Horizons: A History of South Holland's Landscape and People*, Heritage Lincolnshire

Crowson, A. et al (2005), *Anglo-Saxon Settlement on the Siltland of Eastern England*, Lincolnshire Archaeology & Heritage Report No. 7

Hallam, H.E. (1965), *Settlement and Society: A Study of the Early Agrarian History of South Lincolnshire*, Cambridge University Press

Ministry of Agriculture, Fisheries & Food (1983), *MAFF Map C: The Wash - Green Marsh Areas,* MAFF

Robinson, D.N. (2001), *The Book of the Lincolnshire Seaside*, Baron Books, Buckingham

Simmons, I.G. (2015), *The landscape development of the Tofts of south-east Lincolnshire 1100- 1650*, in Landscape History, Volume 36 Issue 1

RIGHT: **Medieval Sea Bank, Fosdyke**

11 : FEN BANKS & DROVES
Medieval Reclamation in the Fens

In the last chapter, we saw how the settlements of the Townlands around the Wash constructed sea banks from the 9th or 10th century onwards to protect themselves from tidal flooding and to expand their farmland by reclaiming estuaries and coastal marshland. The same settlements also built banks for protection against the freshwater fens on their landward side, and likewise expanded their arable land and meadow into the fens using a succession of banks and enclosures in the centuries up to 1300. This chapter focuses on these fen banks, together with the droves and other landscape features that accompanied Medieval fen reclamation.

Origins: the Fens and settlement before embanking

The precise date of the earliest surviving fen banks in Lincolnshire is uncertain, but they are generally accepted as being pre-Norman and were probably constructed during the Anglo-Danish period around the time of the first sea banks. Tracing the emergence of the Medieval fen wetlands and of the settlements which constructed these early banks is therefore

useful. In previous chapters we saw that the Roman Fenland was probably bounded in Lincolnshire by the Car Dyke, with numerous salterns and farming settlements occupying siltlands which extended to the coastline, probably located close to the present-day Townlands. Some peatland existed, but mostly as a narrow belt near the Fen Edges. From the late Roman period, silting of the Wash coastline is thought to have initiated wetter conditions and peatland expansion, as rivers were less able to remove water entering the Fen Basin. At the same time, a marine incursion occurred

157

FACING PAGE: **old fen road or 'gate', Sutton St. Edmund**

RIGHT: **Austendyke, Moulton**

The most extensive Medieval fen reclamation in Lincolnshire occurred south of the Wash in Elloe wapentake, where up to six main fen banks had been constructed by 1300. Today, these can be traced as parallel roads running west-east across the landscape between Spalding and Tydd St. Mary. The earliest of these banks almost certainly predate the Norman Conquest, including Austendyke and Hurdletree Bank. The reclaimed fenland here was used mainly for arable, and by the 12th century the Elloe Townlands were coming into conflict with their neighbours to the south over grazing land, particularly Crowland Abbey, which refused them access to the Crowland fens. Asendyke marked the Medieval boundary between the siltland parishes and Crowland. Later, it became the northern limit of the Bedford Level, as the drainage of Great Postland Fen was linked with Vermuyden's 17th century schemes for the Earls of Bedford. Intriguingly, it may also lie near the frontier between the *Gwyre* and *Spalde* territories of the Anglian Tribal Hidage.

LEFT: **Asendyke, Crowland / Moulton**

FACING PAGE: **Medieval bridge, Crowland**

in c. AD 400 - 500, depositing silts over much of the coastal zone and covering many Roman and prehistoric sites. Nevertheless – contrary to earlier interpretations – site archaeology indicates that the Fens were occupied continuously even after the Romans left (*Hall & Coles, 1994). As the sea receded again, more people settled on the drying coastal siltlands (Cope-Faulkner, 2010). Initially, settlement was dispersed but focused in a clustered pattern along the margins of the emergent fen wetlands, where the risk of flooding was presumably outweighed by the rich natural resources available. However, continued expansion of fen peat pushed settlement away from these early sites. Now divided by a

broad belt of fen wetland, the Fen Edges and the silt 'island' of Holland followed distinct landscape paths. Settlement nucleation occurred on both sides but was earlier along the Fen Edges, where the present villages emerged as early as the 7th and 8th centuries. Around the Wash it occurred later during the Anglo-Danish period, creating the arc of 'primary' villages of the Townlands. Several causeways crossed the Medieval fens (see Chapter 13) but it was not until the post-Medieval period that the Townlands were reconnected to 'upland' Lincolnshire by dry land. Nevertheless, it was in the Medieval period that the reclamation of the fen wetlands commenced.

Bank or dyke? In the Medieval period, the construction of a bank or 'dyke' for flood defence generally involved digging out earth and therefore also created a ditch. The word 'dyke' is found in Old English and – like *dijk* in Dutch – referred originally to the raised bank itself. Subsequently, its use in the Fens transferred to the ditch – usually water-filled – and ultimately to any small drainage channel, whether or not associated directly with embanking. In the Fenland today, 'dike' normally means a small, man-made drainage channel, while larger channels are known as drains. Embankments are usually called banks, though the older form 'dyke' or 'dike' survives in placenames. Some fen banks have lost height over time but most remain in use as roads or paths and many are still above the level of the adjoining fields.

FACING PAGE: **Quadring High Fen from Beck Bank.** Beck Bank is part of the New Fendyke of Kirton (see main text).

RIGHT: **Wrangle Common from Wrangle Bank.** Wrangle Bank is thought to be of Medieval origin, probably pre-Conquest, and was constucted to protect Wrangle's farmland from the East Fen. It forms part of a longer fen bank within Skirbeck Wapentake.

Fen reclamation from the Medieval Townlands

At some time following settlement nucleation, the Townlands saw an increasing desire and/or ability to control their fens and the construction of fen banks commenced. Increasingly, villages acted together to build common fen banks, though patterns of reclamation varied between the area's three wapentakes (Hallam, 1965). The largest area of Medieval reclamation is seen in Elloe wapentake south of the Wash, where a complex succession of fen bank was constructed between the 9th/10th and 13th centuries, and a series of daughter settlements and monastic granges established. Moulton Chapel, Whaplode St. Catherine, Holbeach St. Johns and Sutton St. James were established by the 12th century, followed by Whaplode Drove, Holbeach Drove, Gedney Hill and Sutton St. Edmund. By the 1240s, reclamation had almost reached the Old South Ea – a former course of the River Nene which was confirmed as the boundary between Lincolnshire and Cambridgeshire by a commission

of 1274 (Owen, 1982). Apart from the anomalous Sutton St. Edmund's Common beyond the Old South Ea, this left the Elloe Townlands with a narrow belt of fen, which then persisted until Parliamentary enclosure. As each fen bank was created, the new land was layed out in elongated, ditched fields usually orientated parallel to the bank. At right angles to the bank were the principle drains and access droves. Other lanes or 'gates' connected places. All of these features can be traced in varying degrees in the modern landscape. The fen banks and droves became roads, now mostly tarmacked, while many drains were retained in later drainage improvements The Medieval field pattern has mostly been simplified by amalgamation, but pockets survive in places.

Fen reclamation west and north of the Wash in Kirton and Skirbeck wapentakes followed the same general pattern but was less extensive and involved fewer fen banks. Kirton wapentake has two main Medieval fen banks between Spalding and Donington – Old Fendyke and New Fendyke or New Dyke – dating probably to the 9th century and c. 1200 respectively (Hallam, 1965). Old Fendyke probably continued to Boston but its route is uncertain, while New Dyke clearly does so beside Old Hammond Beck. Daughter villages here include Pinchbeck West, Gosberton Risegate and Kirton Holme. The latter was associated with ditched fields north of Kirton End called 'holmes', which the New Dyke would have protected. Northwards again, Skirbeck wapentake and the adjoining coastal

162

TOP LEFT: **Mole Drove, Gedney Hill**

LEFT: **ditched pasture with cattle, Swineshead**

settlements in Lindsey – Friskney and Wainfleet – have a well-preserved Medieval fen bank which gave protection against the East Fen. Called Ings Bank or Old Fendyke and probably dating to the Anglo-Danish period, it protected low-lying land (Low Grounds) between the East Fen and the Townlands silt ridge, the latter continuing north to Wainfleet as an artificially raised area of saltern waste known as the Tofts. Wrangle has a second bank of probable pre-Conquest date called Gold Fen Dike Bank which retains well-preserved Medieval field patterns, including some 'dylings' (see Chapter 6). At least some parishes in Skirbeck also built an outer fen bank after 1066 to protect new 'ings' of meadowland.

The map overleaf shows the main Medieval fen banks described in this chapter, most of which can still be traced as modern roads and/or ditches. It is worth noting that Medieval reclamation also took place from the Fen Edges of Kesteven and the Wolds, though this was less extensive and generally lacked common fen banks. The Witham Fens below Lincoln saw the creation of banked drains/waterways or 'delphs' together with the Dales Head Dyke, which enclosed reclaimed meadowland plots or 'doles' beside the Medieval River Witham (Hallam, 1965).

By the end of the Medieval period, therefore, significant inroads into the Lincolnshire Fens had been made. Neverthleless, this left a near continuous belt of unreclaimed fenland between the Townlands and Fen Edges. The drainage and reclamation of this area was largely post-Medieval and is explored further in the following chapter.

163

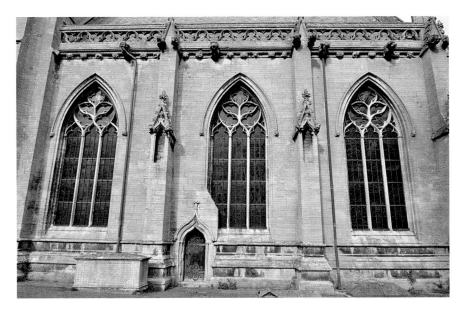

Kesteven Fen Edge: **Billingborough** (TOP RIGHT) and **Heckington church** (RIGHT)

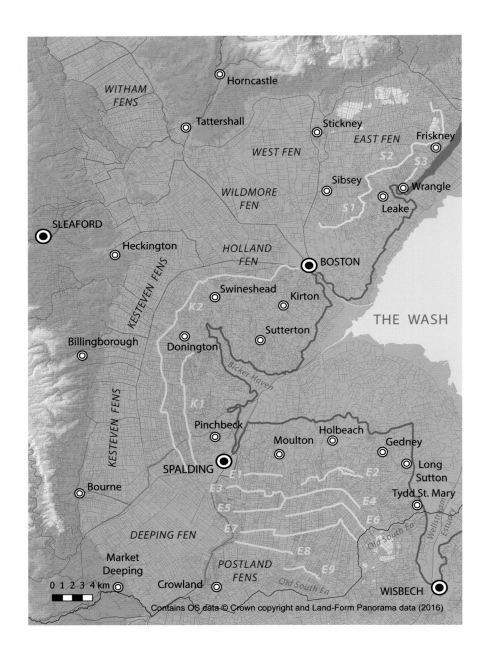

164

The Main Medieval Fen Banks in the Lincolnshire Fens

— fen bank

— Medieval coastline of c. 1300 (= Medieval Sea Bank)

— the Tofts ridge (Wrangle to Wainfleet)

ELLOE WAPENTAKE

E1 - Austendyke *

E2 - Hurdletree Bank *

E3 - Old Fendyke (Spalding to Randall Bank) [early 1100s]

E4 - Saturday Dyke or Raven's Bank [c. 1160-70]

E5 - New Fendyke (Spalding to Randall Bank) [c. 1186-9]

E6 - Hassock Dyke [c. 1190] + Old Fen Dyke (Gedney to Tydd St. Mary) [c. 1190]

E7 - Goldyke + Asgardyke + New Fendyke (Gedney to Tydd St. Mary) [c. 1205]

E8 - Asendyke or Queen's Bank

E9 - Common Dyke (Whaplode to Gedney) [1241]

KIRTON WAPENTAKE

K1 - Old Fendyke *

K2 - New Fendyke / New Dyke [c. 1200?]

SKIRBECK WAPENTAKE

S1 - Ings Bank *

S2 - Wrangle Bank + Fen Bank + Old Fen Bank *

S3 - Gold Fen Dike Bank

* probably constructed pre-1066

Source: Hallam (1965)

References

Cope-Faulkner, P. et al (2010), *Wide Horizons: A History of South Holland's Landscape and People*, Heritage Lincolnshire

Green, T. (2012), *Britons and Anglo-Saxons: Lincolnshire AD 400 - 650*, The History of Lincolnshire Committee, Lincoln

Hall, D. and Coles, J. (1994), *Fenland Survey: An essay in landscape and persistence*, English Heritage

Hallam, H.E. (1965), *Settlement and Society: A Study of the Early Agrarian History of South Lincolnshire*, Cambridge University Press

Healey, H. (1997), *A Fenland Glossary for Lincolnshire*, Lincolnshire Books

Owen, A.E.B. (1982), *A Fenland Frontier: the establishment of the boundary between Cambridgeshire and Lincolnshire*, in *Landscape History*, Volume 4

Simmons, I.G. (2013), *Rural landscapes between the East Fen and the Tofts in south-east Lindsey, 1100 - 1550*, in *Landscape History*, Volume 34, Issue 1

RIGHT: **Beck Bank and Old Hammond Beck, Pinchbeck / Gosberton**

12 : DRAINS & DYKES
Draining the Fens & Carrs

The previous two chapters explored the history of embanking for the reclamation of tidal marshland and fenland in Lincolnshire, focusing on the activities of the Medieval settlements around the Wash. This chapter turns to the other main linear feature employed in the drainage and reclamation of Lincolnshire's wetlands – the drain.

In essence, drains are artificial watercourses that collect and carry water from (or across) low-lying areas to the main rivers or sea, operating in conjunction with pumping stations and sluices to ensure that the land is kept dry enough for agriculture throughout the year. Together with river embankments, washlands and sea defences, drains are integral to an artificial drainage system that has developed over two millennia to prevent flooding and reclaim wetland for farming and settlement.

Despite their apparent mundaneness, drains vary widely in their origins and form. They include both straightened or 'canalised' sections of what were originally natural watercourses, as well as artificial channels on wholly new courses. The nomenclature of drains often reflects this history, as well as their size and purpose. The elements 'ea' (or 'eau'), 'beck' and 'river' are usually indicative of a natural origin. 'Drain' occurs throughout Lincolnshire, while the Fens in particular show a variety of names for drains including 'cut', 'delph', 'grove', 'syke' and 'lode', the latter usually denoting a waterway that gave access by boat. Small field drains are known as 'dykes'.

This chapter explores drains, covering their history and role in the wider landscape development of Lincolnshire's wetlands. The main focus is on

167

FACING PAGE: **Metheringham Delph, Witham Fens**

RIGHT: **River Torne and side drain near Tunnel Pits, Isle of Axholme**

the Fens as the largest former wetland, but reference is also made to other areas including the Isle of Axholme, Ancholme Carrs and Lindsey Marsh.

Early drainage: from the Romans to the Tudors

The emergence of drains is, like many of Lincolnshire's other landscape features, difficult to pinpoint with certainty. The earliest known human intervention for controlling and redirecting water in Lincolnshire relates to salt making and dates to the Iron Age (Lane & Morris, 2001). However, the Romans are usually assumed to be the first significant drainage engineers, with conjectural works including both the straightening and cutting of channels for navigation or improved drainage – though these are rarely backed up by definitive proof on the ground. The probable Roman origin of Car Dyke as a catchwater drain between Peterborough and Lincoln

Many Medieval or earlier drains can still be traced in the landscape, especially where they have continued in use to the present day. In the Fens, Ouse Mere Lode is a notable example which originated as a natural watercourse. The stream rises in the Kesteven Uplands near Folkingham before heading east into the Fens at Billingborough. The artificially straightened course of the 'lode' would have given access to Billingborough village from the *Midfendic* and coast in Medieval times, and possibly earlier from the Roman period. It was also navigable in the 18th century when the Black Sluice Navigation was created. The lode continues across the Medieval fen banks to Quadring, becoming Mar Lode, which originally flowed into the estuary of Bicker Haven.

TOP LEFT: **Ouse Mere Lode, Billingborough, Kesteven Fen Edge**

LEFT: **Mar Lode, Quadring Townland, Fens**

168

was noted in Chapter 5, while Sincil Dyke in Lincoln is often accorded a Roman origin. Contrary to claims by some early historians, however, there is no evidence of a Roman scheme to drain the entire Fens.

Historically-recorded drainage works in Lincolnshire begin in the Medieval period following the Norman Conquest, when major landowners sought protection from flooding and improvement of their lands for agriculture. In the 11th century, the Norman noble Richard de Rulos apparently embanked the River Welland to reclaim part of Deeping Fen for pasture and meadow, and constructed settlements at Market Deeping and Deeping St. James (Wheeler, 1896). Crowland Abbey undertook drainage works in the surrounding fenland, as well as embanking work to the River Welland between Brothertoft and Spalding.

Wheeler's classic text on the Fens otherwise has little to say on Medieval drainage works. It is fairly clear, though, that new drains must have been cut and watercourses straightened as part of Medieval fen reclamation by the Townlands (see Chapter 11). Drains were almost certainly being created in connection with reclamation elsewhere in the Fens too, such as the Dales Head Dyke in the Witham Fens. Hallam (1965) suggests that the 'delphs' of the Witham Fens were in existence before 1300 and were initiated by the monasteries along the Witham valley. In addition to drainage, many straightened channels and cuts were also used for water transport from Medieval times and probably earlier (see Chapter 15).

RIGHT: **Crowland Abbey**

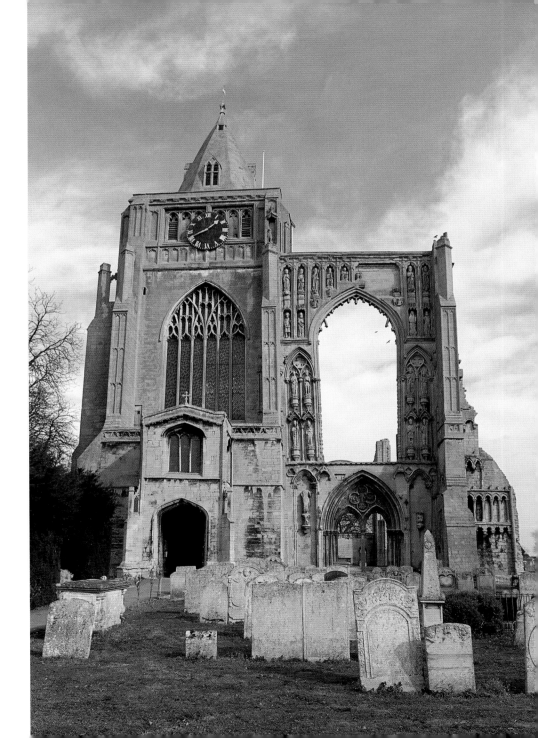

The drainage schemes of the 1600s often employed Dutch engineers and labour for the design and execution of the works. In 1631, Vermuyden undertook to drain Hatfield Chase and the Axholme wetlands for Charles I. He was later contracted by the Earl of Bedford to drain the Bedford Level, though another Dutchman, Philibert Vernatti, was chosen in preference for the related work in the south Lincolnshire Fens.

FACING PAGE: **Delph Drain at dusk, Pinchbeck South Fen**

ABOVE LEFT: **Dutch gable, Epworth, Isle of Axholme**

ABOVE RIGHT: **reeds by River Witham, Washingborough Fen**

Big Drainage begins: adventurers, Dutchmen and dyke wreckers

While Medieval drain-building in Lincolnshire's wetlands was probably more common than historians have generally acknowledged, it was not until the 1600s that schemes for the draining of large areas of wetland began to be implemented in earnest. Reflecting a new, more capitalist and technical approach to land and agriculture, groups of investors called

The embanking of rivers to prevent flooding dates back at least to the Anglo-Danish period, and may have been commenced even earlier by the Romans. From the 1600s, most drainage schemes included embanking and straightening of rivers to remove water quickly towards the coast. In addition, embanked drains were constructed parallel to the main river channels to create washlands for the storage of flood water. The most famous of these are the vast Ouse Washes in Cambridgeshire, constructed as part of Vermuyden's drainage of the Bedford Level. In Lincolnshire, washes were created in the mid 17th century along the Rivers Welland and Glen in connection with fen drainage works in this area. As reclamation of the Fens progressed, the washes became refuges for traditional Fenland activities including wildfowling and ice skating. Use as washlands continued until the 1960s, when pressure for arable saw most of them ploughed up. However, a small area of the Glen or Counter Drain Washes survives as a nature reserve at Tongue End.

LEFT: **willow at Counter Drain Washes, Baston Fen**

FACING PAGE: **River Witham near Five Mile Bridge, Fiskerton**

'adventurers' were now permitted by law to undertake the drainage of wetland commons in return for a share of the reclaimed land.

The wetlands had long seen conflict over ownership and access to land between communities and landowners, as well as disputes about the upkeep and repair of banks, drains and sluices. However, the interests of the Crown and the capitalist adventurers now collided directly with the long-established rights of communities whose livelihoods relied on the wetlands for a range of resources, including grazing, peat, reeds and food

from fishing and wildfowling. Moreover, the adventurers were typically wealthy individuals, often local gentry, whose perspective was radically different from that of subsistence wetland dwellers. The result was nearly two centuries of conflict in which communities sought to prevent fen drainage by legal routes and, when this failed, by direct action. In the Isle of Axholme and Lincolnshire Fens, campaigns by 'dyke wreckers' to sabotage banks, sluices and other drainage works continued into the 18th century, sometimes also involving attacks on crops, livestock, farm buildings and even settlers. Several murders are recorded. Violence had

generally decreased by the 1800s, though opposition to drainage and enclosure remained strong. Despite the ongoing conflict, large areas of Lincolnshire's wetlands were reclaimed in the 1600s and 1700s, albeit with varying degress of success. The main schemes of the 17th century were Vermuyden's reclamation of the Isle of Axholme wetlands (1620s), the Ancholme Carrs (1637) and Vernatti's work in the Deeping, Bourne and Spalding Fens (1630s and 40s). Construction of the South Forty Foot Drain and reclamation of the Earl of Lindsey's Level occurred in the 1630s, but was then abandoned due to sabotage and the Civil War, being redrained later as part of the Black Sluice District. Along with new drains, washes were created to store excess flood water along the Rivers Welland and Glen.

In the 18th century, the main drainage schemes were the reclamation of Holland Fen (commenced 1720s), the straightening and 'improvement' of the River Witham (Act of 1762), drainage of the Black Sluice District (Act of 1765) and the drainage and enclosure of the Witham Fens (1770s).

The reclamation of Holland Fen began in the 1720s with the construction of Lord Fitzwilliam's Drain, later renamed the North Forty Foot Drain. A subsequent Act of Parliament of 1767 authorised the drainage and enclosure of the whole fen. Despite fierce local resistance to loss of the fen commons, the area was transformed into private farmland. In 1812, a church was built to serve the area's growing population.

FACING PAGE: **deserted cottages, Reed Point, Holland Fen**

TOP RIGHT: **interior of All Saints' parish church, Holland Fen**

RIGHT: **remains of scoopwheel, Claydike Bank, Amber Hill**

175

One of the main problems for these early schemes was the lowering of the land surface following drainage, especially in peat areas like Deeping Fen. Increasingly, pumping was required to lift water from the field dykes into the drains and thence into the main rivers. From the 1600s, wind-powered scoopwheels or 'wind engines' became common in the Fens and remained as a feature for two centuries. Sadly, there is no complete wind engine *in situ* in Lincolnshire today, though Dyke Mill was relocated from Deeping Fen in the 1840s and two partial examples survive in Holland Fen. Steam pumping began to replace wind generally from the 1820s, with coal-fired pumping stations being built in the Fens, Isle of Axholme and elsewhere.

The last of Lincolnshire's wild fens

The last main area of unreclaimed fen in Lincolnshire to be drained and enclosed for agriculture lay in the northern Fens – namely Wildmore Fen, West Fen and East Fen. There had been various interventions to improve drainage here over the centuries, including the construction of the Maud Foster Drain in 1568 and Newham Drain from West Fen to Anton's Gowt in the 1630s. Maps from the 17th century also indicate a number of early enclosures in the Wildmore and West Fens, including Medlam (Wheeler, 2008). However, the bulk of these fens were still in use in 1800 as inter-

176

TOP LEFT: **sunset from Westville, West Fen**

LEFT: **Friskney Decoy, East Fen**

commoned grazing that was either seasonally or permanently wet.
The East Fen had a network of interconnected pools or 'deeps' akin to
the Norfolk Broads and similarly created by Medieval peat extraction.
Drainage and parochial partition of these last fens was led by Sir Joseph
Banks of Revesby Abbey with engineering by Sir John Rennie, and was
undertaken from 1803 to 1814 in the face of local opposition. The scheme
included new catchwater drains to intercept upland water and transfer it
to the Witham near Boston. Parish enclosure and new villages followed,
including New Bolingbroke, Westville, Midville and New Leake.

The Fens were not the only wetland area where drainage improvements
continued into the 1800s. Rennie was also involved west of Lincoln, where
new drains were cut in 1804 - 16 to drain low-lying land along the Fossdyke
and Till. In the Ancholme Carrs, Sir John Monson's original scheme had
been sabotaged during the Civil War, but drainage recommenced under an
Act of 1796, which also sought to make the river navigable to Bishopbridge.
Further improvements and river straightening occurred in the 1820s under
the New River Ancholme Drainage Scheme, undertaken by Rennie's son,
also John, including the suspension bridge over the Ancholme at Horkstow.

RIGHT: **Dyke Mill, near Bourne, Kesteven Fen Edge.** This wooden-boarded smock mill
is thought to date originally to the 1700s and was built as a 'wind engine' for pumping
water in Deeping Fen. There were over 50 'wind engines' in Deeping Fen alone by the
early 19th century, though they were rapidly disappearing here and elsewhere in the
Fens by 1850 with the rise of steam pumping. This mill was moved to its present location
in 1845 for use as a corn mill. Sadly, the cap, sails and machinery have not survived.

178

LEFT: **delph with reeds, Witham Fens.** Ironically, many drains now provide an important habitat for species that were found in the fens and carrs before drainage. Increasingly, managment of drains for wildlife is being integrated with their traditional role of removing water.

FACING PAGE: **drain clearance on Fodder Dyke, East Fen.** The construction of drains before the late 19th century was undertaken manually by gangs of drain cutters using only pick, shovel and barrow, while repairs were similarly undertaken by 'banksmen'. By 1900, excavation had largely been mechanised using steam shovels and draglines produced by Ruston of Lincoln and others, followed in the 1930s by diesel models. More recently, modern hydraulic machines have largely taken over the task.

Drainage of the Lindsey Marsh and its valley fens was comparable to that of the Fens, though on a smaller scale and with less severe river flooding. Uniquely, in the Trent Valley and Humberhead Levels, drains were used to2 'warp' land with silt-rich flood water to raise its height and boost soil fertility.

By the 1820s, virtually all of Lincolnshire's wetlands had gone, the only significant exception being the peat 'waste' of Crowle Moor in the Isle of Axholme. However, it was not until the introduction of steam pumping that flooding was eliminated from the drained lands. In the last century, steam pumping was replaced successively by diesel and then electric power.

Today, drains and pumping remain central to land drainage in Lincolnshire, protecting lives, property and farmland. The price paid historically in ecological losses and social strife in the wetlands has been high, however, with the late destruction of the East Fen 'deeps' being particularly regrettable in terms of biodiversity and landscape conservation. Nevertheless, we can still glimpse the untamed fens and carrs along reedy drains and at nature reserves including Baston Fen and Crowle Moor. Recently, too, the Wet Fens Partnership has been established to conserve wetland, including schemes in Lincolnshire and Cambridgeshire to extend fen habitat through the rewetting of land.

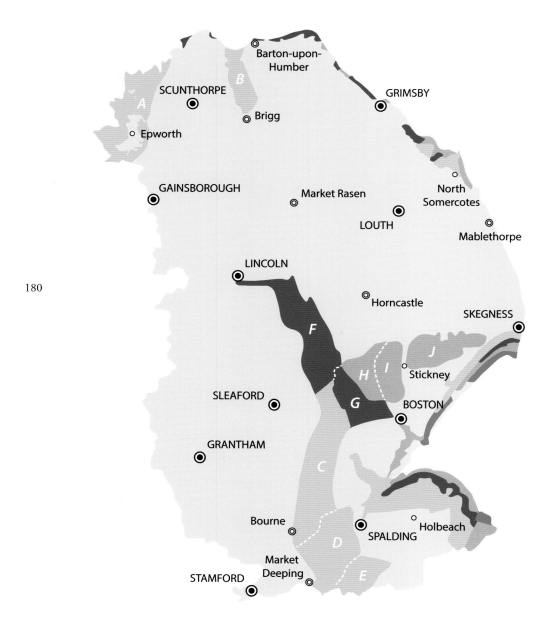

Drainage & Reclamation of Lincolnshire's Wetlands

Post-Medieval reclamation of wetland areas:

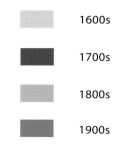

1600s

1700s

1800s

1900s

MAIN FENLANDS OF LINCOLNSHIRE:

A - Axholme wetlands

B - Ancholme Carrs

C - Kesteven Fens (formerly Earl of Lindsey's Level)

D - Deeping Fen

E - Postland Fens

F - Witham Fens

G - Holland Fen (formerly Hauthuntre Fen)

H - Wildmore Fen

I - West Fen

J - East Fen

Source: Bennett & Bennett, 2001

References

Hallam, H.E. (1965), *Settlement and Society: A Study of the Early Agrarian History of South Lincolnshire*, Cambridge University Press

Hills, R.L. (2003), *The Drainage of the Fens*, Landmark Publishing

Lane, T. & Morris, E.L. (eds) (2001), *A Millennium of Saltmaking*, Lincolnshire Heritage

Rotherham, I.D. (2013), *The Lost Fens: England's Greatest Ecological Disaster*, The History Press

Simmons, B.B. & Cope-Faulkner, P. (2004), *The Car Dyke*, Lincolnshire Archaeology and Heritage Reports Series No 8, Lincolnshire Heritage

Van de Noort, R. (2004), *The Humber Wetlands: The Archaeology of a Dynamic Landscape*, Windgather Press

Wheeler, R.C. (ed) (2008), *Maps of the Witham Fens from the Thirteenth to the Nineteenth Century*, The Lincoln Record Society

Wheeler, W.H. (1896), *A History of the Fens of South Lincolnshire*

RIGHT: **field drain or dyke, Tongue End, Deeping Fen**

13 : FEN CAUSEWAYS & WASHWAYS
Traversing the Wetlands & Estuaries

Today, most of us take for granted that roads are available to convey us anywhere within Lincolnshire on a more or less direct route, uninterrupted by wetlands. However, this is a relatively recent development historically, and land travellers before the drainage schemes of the post-Medieval centuries had to contend with extensive areas of fen and carr that were inundated and often impassable, especially in the winter months.

However, efforts to construct dry routes across the Fens have a long pedigree in Lincolnshire, and a number of permanent fen causeways had developed by the Medieval period. Likewise, routes giving relatively safe passage across the tidal estuaries of the Wash had also emerged by this time. This chapter traces the history of these causeways and washways, focusing particularly on routes which persist in the modern landscape.

FACING PAGE: **Nene estuary at dawn.** Before the 1600s, the Nene estuary was several miles wide and extended inland to Wisbech (Cambs). Sutton Washway operated as a guided crossing until the reclamation of Wingland Marsh in the 1820s.

RIGHT: **near Sibsey, Fens.** The area of fenland between Sibsey and Old Leake underwent reclamation in Medieval times. Prior to this, the only dry route availble between Sibsey and the coastal settlements was via the Hilldyke Causeway to Boston.

Prehistoric causeways: pathways to the spirit world?

The buried remains of prehistoric causeways have been discovered in several of Britain's wetlands. Constructed of timber, the earliest known examples date to the Bronze Age, including the remarkable causeway and platform excavated and preserved in the museum at Flag Fen near Peterborough.

184

It seems likely that similar causeways would have occurred elsewhere along fenland edges at this time, especially in Kesteven, though uncertainties remain about their purpose.

Within Lincolnshire, the Witham valley below Lincoln has so far yielded the richest archaeology of prehistoric causeways. At least nine causeways are thought to exist and excavation at Fiskerton indicates them to be of Iron Age origin, related to the development of fen wetland in the valley (Catney & Start, 2003). Based on associated prehistoric finds from the River Witham, archaeologists believe the causeways may have been built to facilitate votive offerings in the river as part of Iron Age spiritual beliefs. It is likely that they also gave access to valley islands and ferry crossing points too.

Later, in the Medieval period, ritualistic offerings continued and became associated with the numerous Christian monastic establishments along the Witham valley. Today, the causeways survive as buried archaeology within the fen deposits and the monasteries are ruins at best, yet these prehistoric routes and sites have influenced the development of the wider landscape over centuries through their ongoing spiritual significance (Stocker, 2006).

Prehistoric timber causeways have also been discovered in the Humberhead Levels at Hatfield and Thorne Moors in Yorkshire though, to the author's knowledge, not within Lincolnshire to date (Plaxton & Graham, 2015).

TOP LEFT: **reeds in the Witham Fens**

LEFT: **Barlings Abbey**

LEFT: **Bridge End Causeway, Horbling Fen.** Bridge End Causeway crosses the Fens between the Kesteven Fen Edge near Horbling and Donington in Holland. The causeway has been attributed by some to the Romans, but this is unsubstantiated and is perhaps unlikely given the geography of the Roman coastline and the subsequent changes in the Fen wetlands. It probably developed (or was consolidtated) as a causeway in the Anglo-Saxon period alongside the nucleation of the Townland settlements and expansion of salt production around Bicker Haven. Nevertheless, the causeway is located inland of the area affected by post-Roman silt deposition and it does directly extend coastward the line of the Salter's Way, which is probably prehistoric in origin. The causeway was apparently the most reliable land route between Kesteven and Holland in the Medieval period and remained so through the turnpike era into the 1800s. The hamlet of Bridge End at the causeway's western end was the site of a small Gilbertine Priory which had responsibility for its upkeep. Today, the causeway carries the A52 and traffic between Grantham and Boston.

185

Medieval causeways: connecting the uplands and Townlands

We saw in Chapter 4 how a regional network of trackways had developed in Lincolnshire by the Iron Age and probably earlier. It is unclear whether substantial causeways were created across Lincolnshire's wetlands in pre-historic times, though this has been conjectured by some. The first clear evidence of causeway construction for more than local use is inevitably Roman. The Fen Causeway branched off Ermine Street north of the Roman town of *Durobrivae* (near Peterborough) and crossed the southern Fens in present-day Cambridgeshire to near Denver in Norfolk. It is thought to date from the mid 1st century and may have been planned as a fast military route to East Anglia in the context of the Boudican Revolt of c. AD60. Evidence for comparable structures has not been confirmed in Lincolnshire to date, though some historians have proposed that Bridge End causeway formed part of a Roman route from the Midlands to the Wash, notwithstanding that the Roman coastline lay closer to the uplands than today. However, as noted in Chapter 5, there is clear evidence for a probable Roman road running between King Street on the Kesteven Fen Edge and the Spalding area – the Baston Outgang. If so, this was probably engineered as a raised road, effectively a causeway, and would have given access to coastal salterns and settlements.

At some time following the establishment of the Medieval Townland settlements around the Wash, causeways developed to connect the area with the uplands for inland trade and travel. These are shown on the map on page 188. Intriguingly, most are still in use today as main roads. Their origins are mostly obscure, though the author has suggested a possible link to the early salt industry for the Bridge End causeway (see Chapter 4).

Washways: on the trail of King John's lost treasure?

Also reflected in the modern landscape are routes that were used to cross the estuaries of the Wash from Medieval times until the reclamation of these areas, some as late as the 1800s. Sutton Wash Way crossed the joint estuary of the Nene and Wellstream (the old Great Ouse), thus linking Norfolk and Lincolnshire. Similarly, the Wash Way crossed the joint estuary of the River Welland and Bicker Haven – the latter being the main estuary of the River Witham until its diversion to Boston in the early 11th century. Shorter routes also crossed each of the main estuary's 'arms' at Cowhurne Droveway and Gosberton respectively.

The form of the washways before reclamation is uncertain, and they may have shifted over time – the modern roads replacing them are almost

certainly straighter. Crossing usually required a local guide, without whom the routes were hazardous. The best-known washway tragedy is that of King John's ill-fated baggage train of 1216 which, if the story is true, probably used the Walpole-Sutton crossing (Waters, 2014). So far the royal treasure has not been located despite concerted attempts to pinpoint the accident.

After centuries of use, the washways were gradually replaced by roads and bridges as coastal reclamation narrowed the old estuaries. Sutton Wash Way, already shortened by marshland reclamation in the 1600s and 1700s, finally gave way to farmland in the 1830s and 40s. The first Cross Keys Bridge over the River Nene was built at Sutton Bridge in 1830 by the local turnpike trust (see next chapter) to a design by Sir John Rennie. Poignantly, the headstone of the last guide to Sutton Wash, Charles Wigglesworth, who died in 1840, is located nearby in the churchyard of St. Mary's in Long Sutton (Waters, 2014).

FACING PAGE: **Church of St. Mary & All Saints, South Kyme.** The South Kyme 'island' site on the edge of the Witham Fens is thought to have been accessed as early as the Bronze Age by causeways linking to North Kyme and Anwick. Continuity of ritual significance at the site is suggested by nearby finds of metalwork including bronze axeheads, which are thought to represent votive offerings. Later, the island became the site of Kyme Priory, a large Augustinian establishment, fragments of which survive in the parish church.

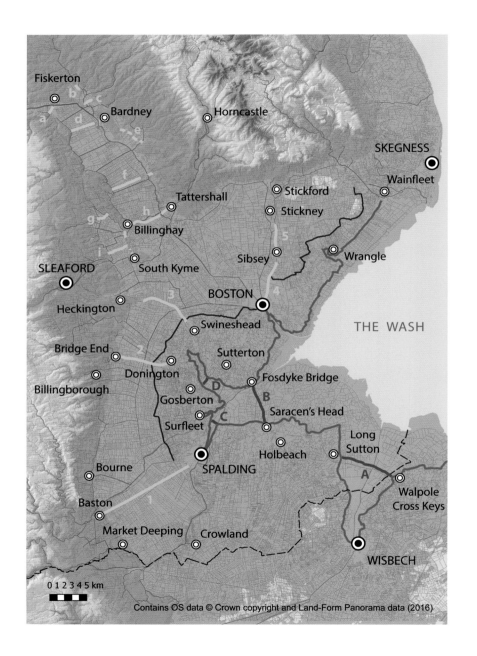

Fen Causeways & Washways in the Lincolnshire Fens

— coastline of c. 1300 (Medieval Sea Bank)

— outer Medieval fen bank (Spalding to Wainfleet)

▬▬ FEN CAUSEWAYS

Causeways in the Witham Fens crossing valley and/or linking 'island' sites:

a - *Fiskerton Causeway [excavated timbers dated to Iron Age, c. 600 BC]*

b - *Barlings Abbey and Short Ferry causeways *

c - *Branston Booths to Bardney causeway *

d - *Tupholme Abbey to Stixwould Priory causeways *

e - *Martin to Kirkstead causeway *

f - *Catley Priory causeway *

g - *Billinghay to Tattershall causeway *

h - *Anwick and Kyme causeways *

Fen causeways connecting to coastal settlements and/or salterns:

1 - *Baston Outgang ***

2 - *Bridge End Causeway*

3 - *Park Dyke Causeway*

4 - *Hilldyke Causeway*

5 - *Nordyke Causeway*

* conjectural Prehistoric causeway, possibly as early as Bronze Age

** evidence for Roman construction

▬▬ WASHWAYS

A - *Sutton Washway*

B - *Wash Way (Holbeach to Fosdyke)*

C - *Cowhurne Droveway*

D - *Bicker Haven Washway*

Source: Catney & Start (2003) and Hallam (1965)

References

Catney, S. and Start, D. (eds) (2003), *Time and Tide: The Archaeology of the Witham Valley*, Witham Valley Archaeology Research Committee

Flag Fen Bronze Age Archaeology Park: The Official Guide,
Jarrold Publishing, 2016

Hallam, H.E. (1965), *Settlement and Society: A Study of the Early Agrarian History of South Lincolnshire*, Cambridge University Press

Plaxton, S. and Graham, T. (2015), *Landscape Conservation Action Plan*,
Isle of Axholme and Hatfield Chase Landscape Partnership

Stocker, D. (2006), *England's Landscape: The East Midlands*,
English Heritage

Waters, R. (3rd edition, 2014), *The Lost Treasure of King John*, Tucann
Books, Washingborough, Lincolnshire

RIGHT: **tidal mudflats in the Wash, the Scalp, Boston**

14 : TURNPIKE ROADS & DROVERS' WAYS
Long-Distance Travel after the Romans

As we saw in Chapter 5, the network of principal roads that existed in Lincolnshire in the Roman period has been identified with reasonable confidence, albeit that some of these almost certainly had prehistoric origins. By comparison, the centuries between the Romans and the emergence of turnpike trusts in the 1600s are relatively obscure. Did travellers simply stick to the old Roman network, as is often claimed, or were new routes created in the Medieval and post-Medieval periods? This chapter investigates the legacy of road travel within Lincolnshire after the Romans left up to the emergence of modern tarmacked roads in the early 20th century. The distinctive legacy of droving is also considered.

Medieval roads in Lincolnshire

Identifying Medieval roads and how they relate to our current network is notoriously difficult, particularly when compared to the engineered routes of the Romans and even, to some extent, the ridgeways of prehistory. Medieval roads were apparently unsurfaced and therefore prone to migrate over time (Hindle, 2016). However, there is both archaeological and historical evidence to help, including early maps and the itineraries of important travellers such as monarchs and bishops. The famous Gough Map of c. 1360 is thought to show the main roads in England with

191

FACING PAGE: **former turnpike road from Wold Newton to Grimsby**

RIGHT: **former droveway, Lincoln Heath**

reasonable accuracy. Surprisingly, only one third of the map's 14th century network of main roads follows routes known to have existed in the Roman period (Roberts, 2002). Furthermore, only three fifths of this 14th century network is then recorded three centuries later by John Ogilvy's map of 1675. Clearly, there were big changes to the national road network during the Medieval and early Modern periods, and road creation appears to have been more significant than is often claimed. In Lincolnshire, we know that Bishop Alnwick (1436 - 39) built 'broad strete' – the precursor of the modern A15 – from Sleaford to Lincoln to facilitate travel between his castle and cathedral (Mills, 2009). The development of causeways across the Fens has already been noted in the previous chapter, while packhorse bridges survive at Scredington, Utterby and West Rasen, reflecting the primacy of packhorses for land transport of wool and other goods in Medieval times.

Nevertheless, it is generally accepted that the condition of roads was poor and deteriorating in Tudor and Stuart times, possibly due to the spread of enclosure confining carriageways between hedges, or simply due to increased traffic. By the 1600s, travellers were desperate for improvements.

TOP LEFT: **Great North Road, Stamford.** As Medieval Stamford developed, the Great North Road was established through the town using this bridging point. The 12th century Town Bridge was rebuilt in 1849, itself probably replacing an earlier, Anglo-Danish one. The Great North Road is still the main road between London and Edinburgh. It follows Roman Ermine Street between Great Casterton (Rutland) and Colsterworth but otherwise had a Medieval alignment in Lincolnshire until the modern bypasses were built at Stamford and Grantham. Ermine Street forded the Welland about half a mile west of here.

LEFT: **14th century packhorse bridge, West Rasen**

Turnpike roads & coaching inns

The establishment of turnpike trusts in England began on the Old North Road (Ermine Street) near London in 1663. Following approval by Act of Parliament, a trust would repair and operate a defined stretch of road, requiring users to pay tolls which were collected at spiked barriers called 'turnpikes'. Turnpiking increased rapidly in the 18th century, and continued until its profitability was undermined by the railways after c. 1850. It is important to note that turnpike trusts in England mostly upgraded and maintained existing roads rather than building new ones (Wright, 1992).

Turnpiking commenced in Lincolnshire on the Great North Road, with new trusts taking on stretches of the latter in 1726 (Grantham northwards) and 1739 (Stamford to Grantham). After 1751, trust formation accelerated, with activity focused in Kesteven in the 1750s and in Lindsey in the mid 1760s. The map on page 200 shows the turnpike roads of Lincolnshire. At the same time, the trusts built toll bridges to replace fords and ferries at Dunham-on-Trent, Gainsborough, Tattershall, Fosdyke and Sutton.

Turnpike roads ushered in the golden age of public stage coaching, which lasted until it was superseded by rail travel in the mid 19th century. Evidence of the coaching era can be found in several Lincolnshire towns and villages which serviced the industry, including the coaching inns with their archways,

RIGHT: **turnpike milestone between Market Rasen and Louth**

yards and stabling. Much of the physical infrastructure associated
with turnpiking was swept away with the demise of the trusts and tolls
from the 1850s, but there are some survivals in Lincolnshire including
mileposts and former till houses (*Wright, 2004). Mileposts or milestones
were made compulsory on turnpiked roads in 1767, though some earlier,
private examples survive. The modern toll bridge at Dunham is a direct
replacement of the original one constructed in the 1830s.

By the 1880s, turnpiking had ceased to operate in Lincolnshire and
the national road network had effectively been rendered redundant by the
railways. Even main roads were essentially for local travel and remained so
until the rise of the motor car in the early 20th century (*Barton, 2016).

Droving & drovers' roads

*At night, the drovers usually sleep only with their cattle, let the weather be
what it will; and many of these hardy men do not rest once under a roof
during a journey on foot from Lochaber to Lincolnshire.*
(The Two Drovers, Sir Walter Scott, 1827)

If turnpike roads and coaching inns evoke images of Georgian panache and
progress, then drovers' roads surely represent the obverse – a romantic

ABOVE: **former droving route along a ridgetop near Hallington, Wolds**

vision of a simple lifestyle spent travelling the ancient byways of England, its unhurried journeys broken only by stops at welcoming wayside hostelries. The reality was, no doubt, often a harsh life exposed to the elements and economic insecurity. Sir Walter Scott's short story was written in the heydey of long-distance droving, when large numbers of cattle were moved commercially from Britain's highlands to the expanding urban centres, above all London. However, droving in the broad sense of people moving livestock across the landscape has a much longer history in Britain, stretching back to the very beginnings of farming.

As noted in Chapter 4, many of the trackways that had emerged in Lincolnshire by the Bronze Age or Iron Age were important for moving cattle, including the Bluestone Heath Road and Sewstern Lane. The latter is still known locally as 'the Drift', an alternative name for a drovers' road. In addition, many local droveways were created and used primarily by local communities for moving their cattle and sheep to and from seasonal grazing land, such as upland pasture or wetland commons, possibly involving transhumance initially. In the Fens, routes that gave access from villages to the common fen before drainage often retain the name 'drove' (see Chapter 11). By Medieval times, livestock were also being moved to nearby market towns and local droving routes became established for this purpose. Fen banks provided convenient routes for droving livestock from Fen pastures to market in Spalding and Boston (*Pryor, 2010).

Moving livestock between Lincolnshire's natural regions represents another category of local droving. The Lindsey Marsh was an important grazing area from at least Medieval times, with considerable movement of sheep and cattle occurring between the Wolds and coastal marshes, the latter often being rented to upland farmers (*Thirsk, 1957). A similar pattern is recorded between the Kesteven Uplands and the Fens. These movements almost certainly developed established routes which offered wayside grazing and convenient stopping points. In the Wolds, droving routes generally followed the high upland ridges, thereby avoiding valley carrs and woods.

From the later Medieval period onwards, long-distance droving became increasingly important, with professional drovers hired to move farmers' livestock to market in London and other cities, primarily from the Scottish Highlands, Galloway and Wales, and also from Ireland. Typically, droves would be divided into stages, the livestock usually being sold on to other drovers to complete the journey to market, and often fattened on route by farmers in places with rich pasture, such as Lincolnshire. The Lincoln to Baumber turnpike of 1739 was apparently established by a group of Wolds farmers to facilitate trade in Scottish cattle which were bought and fattened before being sent for sale in London (*Bennett & Bennett, 2001). This is unusual, though, in that most drovers avoided turnpiked roads and their tolls. Geese were also being driven from Lincolnshire to London in large numbers by the late 1600s, principally from the Fens (*Thirsk, 1957).

As with turnpiking, the majority of routes used by professional drovers were already in existence, including sections of prehistoric trackway, Roman road and other green lanes. As such, it is not always possible to distinguish drovers' roads from other routes. However, there is evidence to help, including placenames and local history (Belsey, 2001). Inn names referring to drovers or livestock offer potential clues, while the name 'drift' occasionally

Lincolnshire's uplands have a long history of droving dating back at least as far as the Iron Age. Both the Jurassic uplands and the Wolds offered convenient ridgeways that facilitated long-distance movement of livestock and were also destinations in their own right for grazing sheep and cattle on their 'heaths' and pastures.

FACING PAGE: **former drovers' road, West Ashby, Wolds.**
The wide verges seen here are characteristic of drovers' roads, though the tarmac strip is of course a 20th century addition.

RIGHT: **cattle on the Wolds near Asterby**

BOTTOM RIGHT: **The Click'em Inn, Swinhope, Wolds.**
This former drovers' inn lies where droving routes converge on the main road between Market Rasen and Grimsby. Paddocks for livestock can still be seen nearby.

survives for green lanes, including one in the West Glen valley near Swayfield and for Sewstern Lane itself. The latter is known to have been part of a long-distance droving route from Scotland and northern England to London, reappearing south of the River Nene in Huntingdonshire as Bullock Road. Sewstern Lane is joined near South Witham by King Street Lane, which crosses the Leicestershire Wolds and was apparently the eastern end of another important drovers' route for cattle movements from North Wales and the North-West (*Barton, 2016). Within Lincolnshire,

Turnpike roads and drovers' routes are often seen as completely separate networks. Coaching companies and their passengers did not want to be held up by large herds of cattle moving at walking pace and probably held snobbish attitudes towards the droving community. Conversely, drovers generally avoided paying turnpike tolls where possible. However, the two worlds did meet sometimes.

LEFT: *The Turnor Arms*, **former coaching inn, Wragby.** The turnpiking of the Lincoln to Horncastle road was instigated by Wolds farmers to attract Scottish cattle droving to the area (Robinson, 2009).

FACING PAGE: **River Witham at Tattershall Bridge.** The original turnpike bridge of 1796 was the only bridge crossing of the Witham between Lincoln and Boston in the early 1800s and was probably much used by drovers. From here, the new turnpike road followed an established droving route west to Sleaford, apart from a section of road built as a shortcut across Kyme Praie Grounds. The surviving common land beside Billinghay Skirth near North Kyme was used by generations of drovers for grazing their cattle and geese.

Armstrong's 1778 map clearly annotates a "*Great Drove Road to Wragby and Horncastle*" between Till Bridge and Scothern, suggesting that a major droving route crossed the Trent at Littleborough (Notts), then followed Tillbridge Lane and Horncastle Lane to Horncastle, presumably en route to the Wolds. Physically too, drove roads may be identified by their width, which can be up to 40 yards (36m) between hedges, or by other features such as pounds and paddocks for holding stock overnight. The planting of Scots pine as a wayside tree to welcome drovers has also been claimed. As with other lanes, the presence of bounding hedges or walls dating to

Parliamentary enclosure does not necessarily mean that a drove road was created at that time; it may simply have been 'formalised' by the enclosure process of tidying up the landscape.

Cattle droving reached its zenith in the period c. 1750 - c. 1850, after which the railways supplanted long-distance journeys on the hoof. Nevertheless, droving was carried on by farmers between farm and railhead until road haulage finally took over in the 1920s and 30s. Today, droving remains as a fascinating if often elusive aspect of Lincolnshire's landscape history.

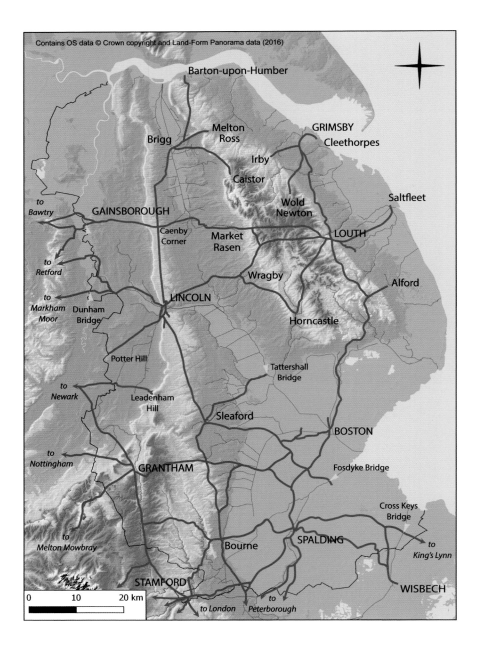

Map of Turnpike Roads in Lincolnshire

——— roads maintained by turnpike trusts in 18th and 19th centuries

➤ toll bridge constructed by turnpike trust

Source: Bennett & Bennett (2001)

References

Belsey, V. (2001), *Discovering Green Lanes*, Green Books, Devon

Hindle, P. (2016), *Medieval Roads and Tracks*, Shire Publications

Howard, J. and Lester, C. (2005) (eds), *Lincolnshire on the Move: Transport in Lincolnshire through the Ages*, Society for Lincolnshire History & Archaeology, Lincoln

Mills, D. (2009), *The Knights Templar in Kesteven*, Heritage Lincolnshire

Roberts, B.K., *Woods, Fens & Roads* in Lane, T. and Coles, J. (eds) (2002), *Through Wet & Dry: Essays in Honour of David Hall*, Heritage Trust of Lincolnshire / Wetland Archaeology Research Project

Robinson, D. (ed) (2009), *The Lincolnshire Wolds*, Windgather Press

Wheeler, R., *Lincoln's Coaching Inns* in Walker, A. (ed) (2015), *Lincoln's City Centre: North of the River Witham*, The Survey of Lincoln

Wright, G.N. (1992), *Turnpike Roads*, Shire Publications

RIGHT: **The Greyhound**, **Folkingham.** Folkingham was a stage post between Bourne and Sleaford on the coaching route from London to Lincoln. In 1788/89, *The Greyhound* was refronted with Georgian brick and 30 stables added. The building was recently converted into residential units.

15 : WATERWAYS
From Freight to Leisure Network

With its broad, lowland rivers and ready access to coastal waters, Lincolnshire has a long history of water transport. We know from finds in the Witham valley that travel by boat was already established in the area by the Bronze Age. It seems likely that movement of commodities by water for exchange and trade has a comparable pedigree.

By the standards of its neighbours, Lincolnshire has relatively few true canals or 'cuts' – these being wholly artificial waterways constructed on new courses independent of existing rivers – but makes up for this with its other waterways. The latter include navigable rivers, mostly improved historically as 'navigations' for water transport, together with artificial drains that also serve as waterways. The map on page 210 shows Lincolnshire's main waterways today, active and disused.

This chapter explores the history of waterways in the Lincolnshire landscape. Medieval waterways are covered briefly, as they have already been discussed under wetland drainage. Lincolnshire's (and Britain's) oldest surviving canal, the Fossdyke Canal, is covered in Chapter 5 given its widely assumed Roman origin.

FACING PAGE: **disused lock, Keddington, Louth Navigation**

RIGHT: **canoeist, Bardney Lock, Witham Navigation**

Early navigation: natural rivers to Medieval waterways

The focus of early water transport was clearly the main rivers giving access from the coast to inland Lincolnshire, including the Humber, Trent, Welland and Witham, as well as several tributaries and smaller streams. By the Iron Age, and probably earlier, established trade routes are likely to have existed using these rivers in combination with trackways. Subsequently, most of Lincolnshire's rivers have been modified by straightening and

embanking to improve navigation and/or drainage (see Chapter 12). As a consequence, Lincolnshire today has little river scenery that can be described as natural and little that would be familiar to our prehistoric or even Medieval boating ancestors. Exceptions include the unnavigable upper reaches of some rivers including the Witham and Glen Rivers in Kesteven and the River Lymn in the southern Wolds. Occasionally, a stretch of 'wild' river remains beside its straighter, replacement channel. Navigation has thus contributed to a transformation of Lincolnshire's watercourses as linear features in the landscape, to which riverine ecology has had to adapt.

The earliest engineering in Lincolnshire to create navigable waterways is generally ascribed to the Roman period. This has already been discussed in Chapter 5, including the possible misattribution of work to the Romans, affecting both Car Dyke and the Fossdyke Canal. The latter, if indeed Roman, is the only extant such canal in Britain. In any case, the improvement of natural watercourses for transport was clearly well underway by the Medieval period, with many new 'lodes' being constructed in the Lincolnshire Fens. Acts of Parliament were passed to regulate trade on several rivers, including the Trent and Witham, covering tolls and horse towpaths, while quays and staithes had been developed on the Trent at Gainsborough by the 14th century, causing a decline in trade at Torksey (Howard and Lester, 2005). However, the improvement of rivers for navigation began in earnest in England in the post-Medieval period,

TOP LEFT: **former Stamford Canal, Uffington**

LEFT: **Old River Bain adjoining Horncastle Navigation, Haltham**

with the first scheme to receive Parliamentary approval being Canterbury in 1515. For Lincolnshire, an Act was passed in 1570 to make the Welland navigable from Stamford to the sea, though work was not completed until 1673. Nevertheless, the extension of the Welland Navigation from Deeping to Stamford is considered by many to be the first 'post-Roman' canal in Britain, and the two former locks at Deeping St. James / Deeping Gate (Cambs) are contenders for the country's oldest navigation locks (*Barton, 2016).

The 'Golden Age' of canals and navigations: 1760 - 1830

The 18th century saw a marked increase in activity to improve Lincoln-shire's waterways for navigation, albeit that some schemes were motivated partly or even principally for drainage. Most improvements involved existing rivers, and are therefore technically called 'navigations' rather than canals. The main commercial navigation schemes undertaken were the Ancholme Navigation (opened 1767), Louth Navigation (part canal) (opened 1770),

Transport on the River Slea dates back several centuries and probably millennia. Historical records show that Gilbert de Umfraville, Lord of Kyme, was involved in a dispute in the 1340s over the right to charge tolls for boats using Kyme Eau, the lower section of the river which was then tidal. By the 1700s, the Slea valley was unnavigable above Kyme and a scheme of 'improvements' including seven new locks was carried out to create the Sleaford Navigation, which opened in 1794. The navigation was profitable until the railway arrived in the 1850s, after which it declined and eventually closed in 1881. Work to restore the navigation has been underway since the 1990s, and the waterway is now navigable again from the Witham as far as **Cobbler's Lock, Ewerby** (RIGHT).

River Glen and Bourne Eau Navigations, Sleaford Navigation (opened 1794) and Horncastle Navigation (opened 1802). The River Witham underwent successive improvements following an initial Act of Parliament in 1762, and is a good example of work concerned with drainage and enclosure as well as transport (Wheeler, 2008). Apart from the Witham, which was connected to the Trent via the Fossdyke Canal, these navigation schemes essentially improved access to Lincolnshire's towns and did not link directly to the wider canal network of the Midlands. However, two canals were constructed between Lincolnshire and adjoining areas in this period: the Grantham Canal (opened 1797) between Nottingham and Grantham, and the Stainforth & Keadby Canal (opened 1802) which linked the lower Trent with industrial south Yorkshire.

A distinctive feature of several of Lincolnshire's waterways is their linkage to the coast or tidal rivers, resulting in the development of tide locks as seen at Boston, Keadby, South Ferriby and Tetney. Consequently, the inland waterways connecting to the Humber estuary and the Wash were used by sailed, sea-going barges called Humber keels and sloops, rather than by conventional canal narrowboats (Taylor, 2003). Alongside the development of Lincolnshire's waterways came new wharves and warehouses, evidence of which can still be seen in several towns.

LEFT: **Bardney Lock, Witham Navigation**

FACING PAGE: **former warehouse, Fen Bridge, Louth Canal**

Reflecting the picture nationally, local enthusiasts have been central to the restoration and revival of Lincolnshire's waterways in the last four decades, leading to a remarkable turnaround in official attitudes to canal heritage.

FACING PAGE: **branch clearance work, Grantham Canal.**
Following its closure in 1936, the Grantham Canal became derelict and was even proposed as a site for tipping. Since the 1970s, however, the Grantham Canal Trust has spearheaded the restoration of the canal for navigation as an ongoing project (see www.granthamcanal.org).

RIGHT: **Humber sloop *Amy Howson* at South Ferriby in 2018.**
The craft that used Lincolnshire's waterways are a key element of its navigation heritage. The Humber Keel and Sloop Preservation Society formed in 1976 and has two restored boats that offer trips on the Humber in the summer months (see www.keelsandsloops.org.uk).

Decline & rebirth: from economic casualty to environmental and social asset

Within fifty years of the 'canal mania' of the 1790s, many of Lincolnshire's waterways were facing their nemesis in the railways, which rendered most water transport uncompetitive. Sometimes, railway companies took over canals, but the decline in the latter was severe and often terminal. Smaller, local canals like the Caistor Canal closed first and by the early 20th century only the larger rivers including the Trent and Witham had maintained their trade. By the 1960s, road haulage finished off what the railways had started and waterways passed into the realm of heritage, much of it derelict and deteriorating. As elsewhere in England, however, the 1950s, 60s and 70s marked a turning point, when voluntary groups and trusts began to restore local canals and waterways for their historical and recreational value. Since then, restoration projects have transformed Lincolnshire's waterways in the context of increasing use for leisure and recognition of their inherent worth. Paradoxically, what commenced with the ecologically insensitive 'canalisation' of rivers for commercial gain has bequeathed us an important environmental asset of great value for wildlife, recreation and tourism, as well as an excellent focus for community participation.

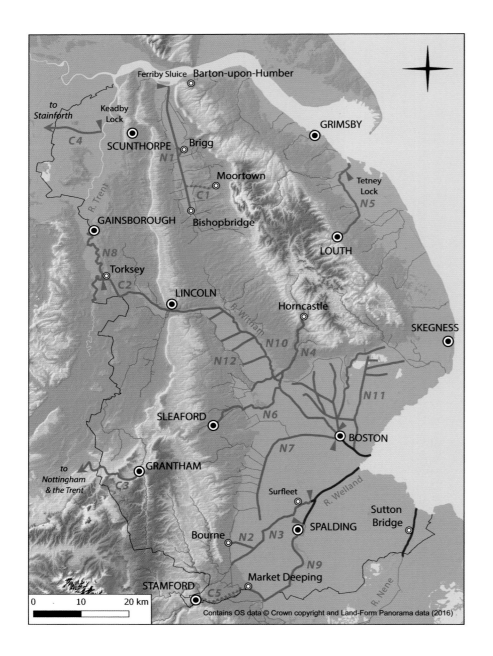

Map of Lincolnshire's Waterways

— tidal river

— inland waterway, extant (navigable / water present)

---- disused canal

► tidal lock / sluice on waterway

CANALS

C1 - Caistor Canal
C2 - Fossdyke Canal *
C3 - Grantham Canal *
C4 - Stainforth & Keadby Canal *
C5 - Stamford Canal

RIVER NAVIGATIONS & NAVIGABLE DRAINS

N1 - Ancholme Navigation *
N2 - Bourne Eau Navigation
N3 - Glen Navigation *
N4 - Horncastle Navigation** and Tattershall Canal
N5 - Louth Navigation **
N6 - Sleaford Navigation *
N7 - Black Sluice Navigation (South Forty Foot Drain)*
N8 - River Trent [Lincolnshire only] *
N9 - River Welland *
N10 - Witham Navigation *
N11 - Witham Navigable Drains *
N12 - Witham Fen Delphs and Billinghay Skirth*

* navigable in full or in part in 2018
** currently unnavigable but restoration proposed

Source: Bennett & Bennett (2001) and Lincolnshire Waterways Partnership

References

Howard, J. and Lester, C. (2005), *Lincolnshire on the Move: Transport in Lincolnshire through the Ages*, Society for Lincolnshire History & Archaeology, Lincoln

Taylor, M. (2000), *The River Trent Navigation*, Tempus

Taylor, M. (2003), *Shipping on the Humber: The South Bank*, Tempus

Wheeler, R.C. (ed) (2008), *Maps of the Witham Fens from the Thirteenth to the Nineteenth Century*, Lincoln Record Society / The Boydell Press

Wright, N., *Navigable Waterways and Canals*, in Bennett, S. and Bennett, N. (eds) (2001), *An Historical Atlas of Lincolnshire*, Phillimore

Note: monographs are available for several of the individual canals and navigations of Lincolnshire, details of which can usually be found on local canal preservation group websites.

RIGHT: **Torksey Lock, Fossdyke Canal**

16 : RAILWAYS
Living Lines and Lost Routes

The cutting of grooves in rock for guiding wheeled vehicles is known to have been utilised in Ancient Greece and Rome. Unlike the man-made lines considered in earlier chapters, however, Britain's railways have no precursor in the landscape before Tudor times at the earliest (see below). Conversely, most railways that remain in use today still employ essentially the same engineering – railbed, bridges, embankments, cuttings, stations, etc – as in their Victorian heyday. Despite the present climate of nostalgia for the age of steam, the railways remain a part of the contemporary landscape of transport in a way that previous technical developments such as stage coaching, macadamised roads and even canals do not.

By the mid 19th century, locomotive rail transport had developed into a revolutionary technological wave sweeping the country with dizzying speed and lasting effect. Railways were both product and creator of Industrial Britain, transforming the economy and society in urban and rural areas alike. Subsequently, the decades from WWI to the 1970s saw successive cuts in the rail network in Lincolnshire as elsewhere, coinciding with the rise of road transport. Today, the closed lines provide a further set of distinctive landscapes with their own ecology and archaeology, some now remodelled for recreational use as cycle routes, paths and linear artscapes.

This chapter looks at the legacy of the 'railway age' in the Lincolnshire countryside today, including their early history as 'tramroads', as well as related impacts on the landscape that encompass patterns of farming and industry, and other changes such as the massive expansion of holiday resorts on the coast.

213

FACING PAGE: **railway bridge view, Wickenby**

RIGHT: **disused Horncastle branch line, Thornton**

Tramroads & early railways in Lincolnshire

While Britain's railways have no precedent in Medieval or earlier times, they do have their own 'prehistory', given that rail technology evolved from industrial wagonways dating back as far as the 16th century. These developed primarily to convey coal and other minerals from mines to navigable rivers or the sea. They typically operated as gravity inclines with horses used to pull the empty wagons back uphill. Various systems were used to keep the wagons on wooden plankways or rails, and flanged wheels had apparently emerged in north-east England by the 1670s. The use of wagonways – often referred to as 'tramroads' – expanded considerably during the canal era of the late 18th century, when they facilitated greatly increased mining activity and early industrial expansion. The earliest known tram-road in the East Midlands conveyed coal from Strelley to Nottingham and was constructed in 1604 (*Barton, 2016).

Lincolnshire lacked early tramroads, as it had no coal mining and began the industrial extraction of minerals such as ironstone somewhat later. However, an important early example adjoined Lincolnshire on the Belvoir estate, where the Duke of Rutland commissioned a tramroad in 1791 to carry coal and other supplies from the new Grantham Canal to his hilltop Castle, a canal branch being impractical here. The horse-drawn tramroad was a technological hybrid which combined elements from James Outram's 'plateway' system and William Jessop's 'edge rails', the latter being the precursor of modern rails that Jessop first developed on tramroads in the 1790s (Hewlett, 1935). The Belvoir Castle tramroad commenced operation in 1815 and remained in use until c. 1918, bringing supplies directly into

214

Despite the apparent timelessness of its landscape, the Belvoir estate (Leics / Lincs) played a significant part in the early development of Britain's railways. Engineered by William Jessop (1745 - 1814), the Belvoir Castle tramroad was one of the first to use his cast iron 'edge rails' rather than iron plates to guide its horse-drawn wagons. The route of the tramroad can still be traced between the Castle and Muston Gorse on the Grantham Canal, lying just outside Lincolnshire. Further tramways were developed in connection with ironstone extraction in the Belvoir area from the 1870s, including one in Lincolnshire at Brewer's Grave (Woolsthorpe / Denton). This used an incline to carry ore down to GNR's Woolsthorpe Branch railway until c. 1918, after which it was dismantled (Hewlett, 1935). The branch line itself closed when quarrying ceased in the 1930s, but its route survives today as a permissive footpath and cycle route, as seen here **near Woolsthorpe Wharf** (ABOVE).

OPPOSITE PAGE: **former weigh house of Lord Willoughby's railway, Edenham**

the Castle, including coal from the Duke's mines in Derbyshire. The route can still be traced as embankments or terracing for most of its length from the former canal wharf at Muston Gorse (Leics). A wagon from the tramway is held at the National Railway Museum in York, where it is billed as "*the oldest vehicle with flanged wheels to be preserved in Britain*" (*Barton, 2016). Intriguingly, the tramroad's construction is broadly contemporary with the rebuilding of the Castle in Romantic Gothic style and the post-humous implemention of 'Capability' Brown's landscaping proposals of 1780 for the Belvoir estate (see Chapter 9).

The development of the iron rail was followed in the early 19th century by steam locomotion, leading to an early, pre-Victorian era of mainly private railways serving industry. This was prior to the spread of Britain's main line railways in the 'railway mania' of the 1840s. Again, Lincolnshire's largely rural economy meant that it lacked such early railway development.

Private railways did develop in the county later, but they were generally linked to existing main lines from the outset. One interesting example is that of the Edenham & Little Bytham Railway, privately built by Lord Willoughby de Eresby on his Grimsthorpe estate. This commenced in 1851 - 3 as a tramway with wagons hauled by a flat-wheeled traction engine, later converting to a railway with flanged wheels and carriages. The system connected to the GNR's main line at Little Bytham and brought coal to the estate as well as being available for passenger travel. Lack of investment led to closure of the line to passengers in the 1860s, with freight ceasing in the 1870s when the line was closed (Pearson & Ruddock, 1986). Parts of the former line can still seen from public footpaths near Grimsthorpe Park.

The construction of Lincolnshire's rail network

If early railways were important in facilitating Britain's Industrial Revolution in the coalfields, the construction of the main line railways in the mid 19th century was a socio-economic tsunami that swept across the whole nation, transforming urban and rural areas alike. Between the late 1840s and the 1880s, Lincolnshire gained most of its main and branch line railways, with two main companies dominating the creation and running of the network until the restructuring of the early 20th century. The Great Northern Railway (GNR) was the key player in central and southern Lincolnshire, and the Manchester, Sheffield and Lincolnshire (MSLR) – later Great Central Railway – in the northern half of the county. The map on page 226 shows the extent of the public railway network by 1914 and the status of these lines today.

Full accounts of the progress of railway building in Lincolnshire can be found in literature on the subject (see Stennett, 2016), but are worth outlining here. Lincolnshire's first main line railway was the Midland Railway's line through Stamford, followed by its Nottingham to Lincoln railway, both opened in 1846. Paradoxically, this company then played a relatively minor role within Lincolnshire. Perhaps the key rail development

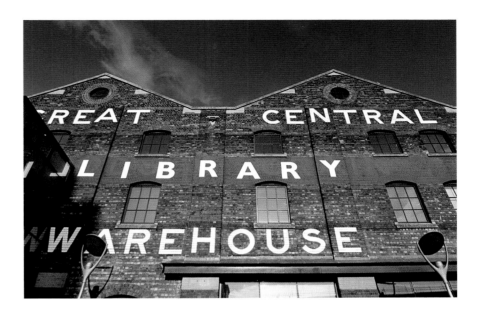

FACING PAGE: **railway bridge on Lincoln to Grimsby line, Wickenby**

TOP RIGHT: **former Great Central Warehouse, now Lincoln University Library**

RIGHT: **steel and stone detail, Torksey Viaduct**

affecting Lincolnshire was the main north-south route through the county in the context of travel between London and the North. The scheme that ultimately triumphed was the GNR's 'Towns Line' from Peterborough to Doncaster via Grantham, cutting and tunnelling a direct route through the Oolite uplands of Kesteven. This ultimately became part of the East Coast Main Line we know today. However, there was an earlier GNR route – the so-called 'Loop Line' – which opened in 1848/49 from Peterborough to Retford (later Doncaster) via Spalding, Boston, Lincoln and Gainsborough. This was an easier route topographically, utilising the Lincoln Gap, but longer and more distant from the industrial areas of the Midlands. Nevertheless, the 'Loop Line' survived in its entirety until the Beeching era and the towns on its route developed further as important railway centres as new lines were added to the network. Sleaford hit the railway map in the 1850s with the opening of the GNR's Boston, Sleaford & Midland Counties Railway.

In north Lincolnshire, the railways focused from the outset more on east-west connectivity, principally between Lincolnshire's coastal ports and the coalfields and towns of Yorkshire and the Midlands. The MSLR's line from

218

Level crossings are still a regular feature on many of Lincolnshire's railways, especially in the flatter areas such as the Fens and Marsh. GNR's East Lincolnshire Railway was particularly noted for the number of such crossings, the cost of maintaining which is said to have contributed to the line's demise in the Beeching era.

TOP LEFT: **architectural detail of former GNR station, Sibsey**

LEFT & FACING PAGE: **level crossings on the former East Lincolnshire line**

Railway children? Not everyone uses trains today, yet we all live in a world transformed economically and socially by the railways. The physical legacy of the railway age is all around us, now familiar enough to be overlooked or framed as nostalgia. Yet if we imagine Lincolnshire before the railways, it is still possible to recapture something of the heady mix of excitement and fear that accompanied the arrival of the first steam locomotives and the unprecedented opportunities they brought for fast travel and new destinations.

FACING PAGE: **bus stop ladies by The Station Inn, Habrough**

RIGHT: **former Rippingale station and present owner.** The station dates to 1879 but became redundant with the closure of the Sleaford to Bourne line to freight in 1965. The building has been lovingly restored by a Lincolnshire railway enthusiast and is now a private residence. The present owner, Marc Maitland, is strongly committed to maintaining the character and railway heritage of the site.

Lincoln to Grimsby opened in 1848, followed by Gainsborough to Grimsby in 1849. The MSLR also built new docks at Grimsby in 1852, though the town's rapid Victorian growth was probably due as much to the expanded market for fish that the railways created (*Bennett & Bennett, 2001). The MSLR added new lines to serve industrial and urban development at Scunthorpe and Immingham, as well as to Cleethorpes where it invested heavily in the town as a holiday resort. The Lancashire, Derbyshire and East Coast Railway of the 1890s was a late example of a coal-focused railway, though the planned continuation east of Lincoln to a new coal port at Sutton-on-Sea never materialised.

Two joint lines developed in Lincolnshire following attempts by other rail companies to expand into the county – the Midland & Great Northern Joint Railway from Bourne to Sutton Bridge, connecting to King's Lynn, and the Great Northern & Great Eastern Joint Railway from Doncaster to March via Lincoln, Sleaford and Spalding. Many branch lines were built by local companies and subsequently taken over by the two main companies.

One late railway outside the two big players was the Isle of Axholme Light Railway, built in 1902 - 08. This was important in transporting the produce of the area's peat industry and farming, particulary celery (Stennett, 2016).

Another important driver of railway growth was the demand for day trips and holidays to the coast from the second half of the 19th century, as the introduction of paid annual leave and bank holidays combined with generally increasing prosperity to bring these within reach of the urban working class. Lines were built or extended to Cleethorpes (1863), Skegness (1873), Mablethorpe (1877) and Sutton-on-Sea (1888), ultimately changing the face of Lincolnshire's coastline as the resorts expanded.

Lincolnshire's wider economy was also transformed by the railways, including its agriculture. Drastically reduced journey times allowed cash crops and horticultural produce to be grown for regional and national distribution, notable examples being Lincolnshire potatoes and cut flowers from the Spalding area. New and expanding industries now moved most raw materials and products by rail. Bass Maltings at Sleaford are a particularly impressive example of railway-based development from the early 1900s, processing Lincolnshire barley for their brewery at Burton-on-Trent.

Mineral lines and potato railways

Despite its relatively late start, Lincolnshire saw the development of several purely industrial railways from the 1850s onwards, primarily for ironstone extraction. Private branch railways were built by mining companies around Scunthorpe, at Nettleton and Claxby in the Wolds and along the border

LEFT: **former peat railway, Epworth.** This branch line of the Isle of Axholme Light Railway mainly carried peat extracted from Hatfield Moor (Yorks). It closed in 1963.

with Leicestershire near Woolsthorpe-by-Belvoir, Harlaxton and Colsterworth. Some of these were still operating in the 1970s, supplying ore to the British steel industry. Beyond the main branch lines, railways were also used to access and extract individual areas, some initially being horse-drawn. A number of Lincolnshire's main lines also served partly to open up new areas for ironstone mining, notably the Lincoln to Honington line of 1867 and the Bourne to Saxby (Leics) line of 1894.

Light railways were employed in agriculture by a number of Lincolnshire farming estates after WWI. The majority were located in or near the Fens, including Nocton, Fleet and Dawsmere, and were particularly associated with potato cropping (Squires, 2005). Most of the railways were horse drawn and carried the potato crop from the fields to storage and loading facilities. Transhipment was mainly to road haulage, though use of main line railways and even barges also occurred. Today, potato railways have disappeared from Lincolnshire's countryside and few have left visible traces. However, the routes of some mineral branch lines can still be followed, including the Woolsthorpe Branch Line near Belvoir.

Railway stations were common in rural Lincolnshire until the 1960s, when the majority were closed, variously being reused, demolished or simply left derelict.

TOP RIGHT: **waiting room at Clifton-on-Trent station.** This abandoned station building is a poignant reminder of the former Lancashire, Derbyshire & East Coast Railway and is built in the company's distinctive style. It lies just outside Lincolnshire, but once served nearby villages within the county.

RIGHT: **Rippingale station.** A unique station refurbishment complete with track.

223

Lost lines and new uses

The 20th century saw big changes in Lincolnshire's railways. Contraction of the network started in the 1920s as road transport took away passenger and freight trade, and accelerated in the 1950s (Stennett, 2016). The 1960s and 70s saw the closure of several lines following Dr. Beeching's infamous 'Reshaping' plan of 1963, including most of the East Lincolnshire Railway and the old GNR 'Loop Line'. Passenger line closures had ended by 1970, though the Spalding to March line was a late casualty in 1985.

The legacy of the cuts has been mixed. Some of the former network has simply disappeared into the landscape or been built on with an apparent disregard for its strategic potential. Many Lincolnshire towns and villages have been left more isolated and with longer journey times to London than 100 years ago. Conversely, closed lines have provided new opportunities for wildlife and recreation. Several abandoned routes have developed into linear nature reserves, enhancing and linking biodiversity in both rural and urban areas. In recent years too, disused railways have increasingly been recognised as an important leisure and transport resource. Routes such as the Water Rail Way are now popular with cyclists and walkers seeking contact with nature in a safe, traffic-free environment, offering positive visions for the future.

FACING PAGE: **disused Bourne to Spalding line crossing the Counter Drain**

RIGHT: **cyclist on the Water Rail Way, Washingborough Fen**

225

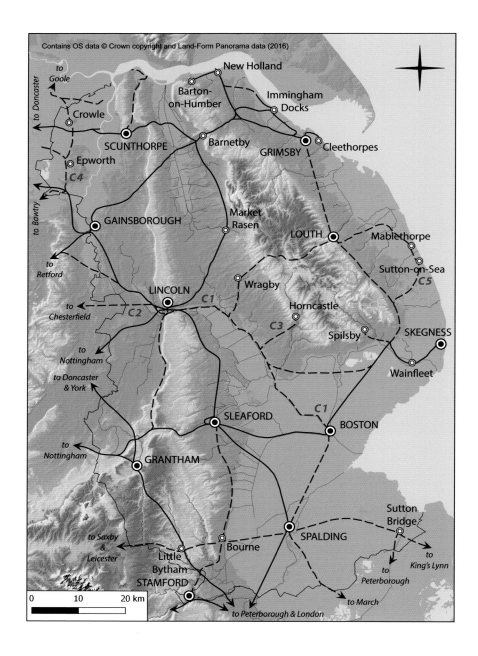

Contains OS data © Crown copyright and Land-Form Panorama data (2016)

Map of Lincolnshire's Railways

The map illustrates the rail network at its maximum extent (c. 1914):

—   lines still in active use as railway today

– –   lines closed since 1914 *

*   *Note: a stretch of the former East Lincolnshire Railway has been reopened as a steam*
     railway between Ludborough and North Thoresby, called the Lincolnshire Wolds Railway

LINES REUSED AS CYCLEWAYS & RECREATIONAL ROUTES:

C1   *WATER RAIL WAY: sections of the former GNR 'Loop Line' now form part*
      of the Water Rail Way between Lincoln and Boston. They are Lincoln to
      Kirkstead Bridge and Langrick to Boston. The Water Rail Way is also
      part of National Cycle Network (NCN) Route 1

C2   *LINCOLN TO FLEDBOROUGH: the former Lancashire, Derbyshire*
      & East Coast Railway between Lincoln and Fledborough Viaduct (Notts)
      now forms part of NCN Routes 64 and 647

C3   *SPA TRAIL: the former Horncastle & Kirkstead Branch Railway is now*
      an off-road recreational route for walkers, cyclists and horse-riders
      between Woodhall Spa and Horncastle. The route also forms part of the
      Viking Way long distance footpath

C4   *ISLE OF AXHOLME GREENWAY: a section of the former*
      Isle of Axholme Light Railway from Haxey to Crowle is proposed
      as an extension of the area's Greenway route

C5   *SUTTON BRANCH LINE WALKWAY & CONSERVATION AREA: a 1.5 mile section*
      of the former Sutton Branch line south of Sandilands is open to walkers

Source: Bennett & Bennett (2001), Stennett (2007) and Sustrans

References

Hewlett, H.B. (1935, reprinted 1979), *The Quarries: Ironstone, Limestone and Sand*, Market Overton Industrial Railway Association, Cottesmore

Pearson, R.E. and Ruddock, J.G. (1986), *Lord Willoughby's Railway*, Willoughby Memorial Trust

Squires, S. (2005), *The Lincolnshire Potato Railways*, The Oakwood Press

Stennett, A. (2007), *Lost Railways of Lincolnshire*, Countryside Books

Stennett, A. (2016), *Lincolnshire Railways*, The Crowood Press, Wiltshire

Tonks, E. (1991), *The Ironstone Quarries of the Midlands: History, Operation & Railways – Part VIII South Lincolnshire*, Runpast Publishing

White, P.R. (1989), *Roads Replace Railways* in Mills, D. (ed) (1989), *History of Lincolnshire Volume XII: Twentieth Century Lincolnshire*, Society for Lincolnshire History & Archaeology

Note: monographs are available for most of Lincolnshire's railways, including A.J. Ludlam's titles for the Oakwood Press and those by the Middleton Press in their Main Lines and Branch Lines series

RIGHT: **exterior detail, The Station Inn, Habrough**

17 : INDUSTRIAL LINES
Mineral Extraction, Milling & Manufacturing

As a rural county with a strong reputation for agriculture, the industrial heritage of Lincolnshire is often overlooked. However, industrial activity has been a part of the landscape since prehistory, when metal working and salt making began, and has added to Lincolnshire's archaeology and built heritage in every period since then to the present day. Classic landscapes of the Industrial Revolution also occur but are are largely restricted to Lincolnshire's northernmost quarter, including Scunthorpe with its iron and steel heritage and the varied past and present industries fringing the Humber, including tile making, food processing and petrochemicals.

In this chapter, we are concerned with lines in the landscape that have resulted from this industrial activity, including mineral extraction, milling and manufacturing. Not all of these have left features of strictly linear form, but they mostly occupy sites or zones bounded clearly by the extent of the activity. In some cases like peat cutting and ironstone quarrying, these zones can be linear. From the 1800s onwards, industrial activity is increasingly connected with new transport developments, particularly canals and railways, which have been considered in previous chapters.

FACING PAGE: **chalk quarry, South Ferriby, Wolds**

Prehistoric & Roman industries: peat, salt and quarries

Industrial activity before the Medieval period is one of the most intriguing aspects of Britain's early landscape development. It has to be said, in Lincolnshire at least, that visible remains do not form a significant element in today's countryside, either as linear features or otherwise. Much of the pre-Medieval land surface in the former wetlands and coast has been covered by later deposits – peat in the inner Fens and marine silts around the Wash and Lindsey Marsh coastlines. Thus, remains of early peat extraction and salt making tend to be buried, including Lincolnshire's fascinating early salterns of Bronze Age to Roman date. One exception, however, are the Romano-British turbaries (peat workings) in the Kesteven Fens near Bourne, where parallel lines created by peat extraction can be detected from the air (Malone & Williams, 2005). Much more extensive examples occur in the peat fens in Cambridgeshire, where they are thought to have supplied both domestic use and salterns (*Hall & Coles, 1994).

In the uplands, too, extraction of building stone and iron ore in this period is mainly obscured by later activity. This includes the probable limestone quarries of the Greetwell area, from which the major buildings and walls of Roman Lincoln were constructed.

Medieval and later peat digging: turbaries and 'ribbons'

By Medieval times, peat extraction in the wetlands was generally controlled as an important community resource with defined common rights. However, Medieval workings could be substantial, as seen in the creation of the East Fen Deeps, themselves now lost to drainage (see Chapter 12). In the Isle of Axholme, distinctive patterns of peatland use and settlement emerged in the post-Medieval period following the draining of the area by Vermuyden. As compensation for the loss of wetland commons a number of turbaries were created in 1803 for the Isle's main villages, including a single turbary each for Haxey and Owston and two each for Epworth and Belton. In the 19th century, small plots of land on these were rented to the parish poor, who built cottages there and supported themselves with livestock, crops and the digging of peat and sand.

A different pattern of settlement is seen on Thorne Moors, where individual settlers established elongated plots extending back into the peatland from the peripheral roads, probably dating originally to the legal disafforestation of Hatfield Chase in the 17th century. These parallel moorland allotments, known as 'cables' or 'ribbons', occur widely in the Yorkshire portion of the moors and can also be seen at Crowle Moor in Lincolnshire. The settlers are thought to have lived by peat-cutting and farming on the plots (Plaxton & Graham, 2015). From the mid 1800s, peat companies began forming to extract and mill peat for a wider market, initially for 'moss litter' and fuel, then for horticultural use.

LEFT: **narrow moorland plot, Ribbon Row, Crowle Moor**

Cutting of peat was by hand until the 1960s when mechanised block-cutting began, though techniques differed between companies and over time, reflecting Dutch, English and Irish workforces. Industrial peat extraction occurred on Crowle Moor from at least the 1890s, but remained distinct in scale and pattern from the Yorkshire moors. Crowle Moor's ribbons survived as units and while more systematic extraction did take place using tramways, similar to those on Thorne Moors, the grid of Dutch peat canals seen on the latter is absent (Limber, 2011). The entire area of moorland now forms the Humberhead Peatlands National Nature Reserve following the cessation of peat extraction in 2005, though evidence of former peat cutting and tramways survives widely.

Salt production after the Romans: saltern mounds and the Tofts ridge

If the prehistoric and Romano-British salt industry lies buried, that of the Medieval period and after occupied the present land surface of coastal silt and even contributed locally to the latter in the forms of low hills of waste generated by the salt extraction process. The saltern buildings disappeared long ago when production ceased in the 1600s, but 'salt hills' remain as a feature of former coastlines. Around the Wash, they occur extensively at Gedney Dyke, Holbeach Hurn and Bicker Haven. Between Wrangle and

Medieval salt production around the Wash has left a curious legacy in the form of hills of silt waste. These have long been converted to farmland, as in these two examples **near Gedney Dyke** (TOP RIGHT) and in **Bicker Haven near Donington** (RIGHT).

Wainfleet, salt mounds form a continuous line of low hills called the Tofts, which probably developed outside an early Medieval sea bank and may have taken over the role of sea defence in the Medieval period. The Geological Survey records the Tofts ridge as being at least partly of natural origin as a storm beach, but this is challenged by some researchers who suggest the feature may be entirely the product of saltern waste (Simmons, 2015).

In the Lindsey Marshland, Medieval saltern waste is thought to have consolidated parts of the coastline for settlement and farming, with a gradual seaward shift in salt production leading to linear patterns of mound creation, land reclamation and field development (Robinson, 2001).

Milling and manufacture in the countryside

On first sight, mills and factories in the countryside form points of activity rather than lines. However, their distribution is often linear, reflecting topographic features and the associated flows of water and air that provided power in the era before steam engines and coal reached Lincolnshire. Thus, watermills occurred along the river network and windmills were often situated on escarpments and ridges. Ellis Mill in Lincoln is the sole survivor of at least eight windmills situated here on the Lincoln Edge in the 1840s.

LEFT: **Mount Pleasant Mill, Kirton-in-Lindsey.** A well-preserved tower mill of 1875 located on the breezy Lincoln Edge. The mill is still working and produces organic flour.

FACING PAGE: **oil refinery on the Humber Bank, Killingholme**

232

Some milling and maunfacturing has left its own lines too. Watermills have artificial mill races and in some cases occupy alternative river channels which were created to avoid interfering with navigation. Later, with the Industrial Revolution, major developments such as Scunthorpe's steelworks and the docks and refineries at Immingham incorporated their own railway systems and sidings, and were laid out in patterns which reflected these.

Extractive industries: stone, clay, iron ore and sand

The main minerals extracted historically in Lincolnshire include building stones, brick clay, iron ore ('ironstone'), limestones and chalk for lime, and sand and gravel. Each of these has its own history and geography within the county, the scale of production typically reaching a peak during the

Industrial era of the 19th and 20th centuries. Coal has never been mined in Lincolnshire, although there were proposals to do so in the 1980s in the 'Witham Prospect' (*Bennett & Bennett, 2001). Today, extraction of minerals continues in some of these sectors, including limestone, chalk, and sand and gravel. There is also localised oil and gas extraction, and fracking proposals appear to have strong support from the present Government.

The pre-Industrial legacy of extraction is mostly small-scale, with quarries for building stone, lime and clay supplying local needs. In some cases, later expansion has destroyed the early archaeology but small, disused quarries and pits can still be traced in the landscape. On the Jurassic Oolite ridge, larger quarries for building stone existed from at least Medieval times, including Ancaster, Clipsham (Rutland) and Barnack (Northants),which supplied high quality stone over a wide area of eastern England. Active

FACING PAGE: **former limestone quarry, Kirton-in-Lindsey.** This vast quarried area supplied limestone and shale to the adjacent cement works between 1920 and the 1970s. The works were opened originally by the Caustic Lime and Macadam Company and passed through several owners prior to closure in 1976. The site is located where the former Manchester, Sheffield & Lincolnshire railway of 1848 cuts through the Jurassic Oolite ridge, and used rail to transport its products. The chimneys on the horizon belong to Glanford Power Station in Brigg.

RIGHT: **tile works, Barton-upon-Humber.** This active tile works now imports clay for its kilns, and the local clay pits that one supplied Barton's tile making industry are now an important resource for wildlife and recreation. Several of the water-filled pits are managed by Lincolnshire Wildlife Trust as local nature reserves, including Far Ings and Barrow Haven.

stone quarries remain in Lincolnshire at Ancaster and Holywell, but quarrying of Jurassic limestones on a much larger scale is now associated mainly with the production of aggregate and lime. Several sites are active today, while others have left extensive, scarred landscapes, as at Kirton-in-Lindsey. Chalk is also quarried in Lincolnshire as a secondary aggregate and for industrial production of lime and cement.

Extraction of clay for brick and tile making was once widespread across the county, but had ceased by the 1980s. As with quarrying, local pits can often still be located. On a much larger scale, flooded clay pits form a continuous linear zone along the Humber Bank between Barton and Goxhill, and formerly supplied the area's extensive tile and brick making industry.

The extraction of 'ironstone' in Lincolnshire is apparently of Romano-British and probably earlier origin, but it is the period after 1850 that saw quarrying and mining develop on an industrial scale in concert with railway building and the creation of Scunthorpe as an iron and steel town. The main sources were in the Jurassic belt around Grantham and Colsterworth, with smaller mining operations in the Wolds near Nettleton. All had closed by 1980, leaving a landscape legacy which is probably of

236

greater appeal to the industrial archaeologist than to most countryside lovers. However, backfilling and restoration to farmland has occurred widely, leaving relatively few traces apart from a land surface below the level of the roads, as around Belvoir and Harlaxton. The archaeology of ironstone quarrying and mining includes occasional quarry structures and workers' housing as well as former branch railway lines (Squires, 2017; Tonks, 1991).

The final mineral activity with major significance for Lincolnshire's landscape is that of sand and gravel extraction. This mainly supplies aggregate for construction and has impacted heavily on several parts of Lincolnshire since the early 20th century, including the Vale of Trent and Bain valley near Woodhall Spa. Clearly, extraction transforms the pre-existing rural landscape in a destructive way and can be environmentally unattractive, especially while active, though the industry's legacy of disused pits also includes valuable new wildlife habitats, including the well-known nature reserve at Whisby near Lincoln.

LEFT: **former sand quarry, Messingham, Vale of Trent.** As late as the 1950s, this area of Coversands formed part of a remarkable and extensive heathland landscape that also included parts of Manton and Twigmoor parishes. Despite having England's finest surviving inland dune systems, high ecological value and SSSI status, destruction and fragmentation occurred through the 1960s and 70s due to agricultural reclamation and sand extraction. The area's regrettable saga is recounted by the late Ted Smith of Lincolnshire Wildlife Trust in his 2007 memoir. Sand extraction continues in the Messingham area, but the naturalised extraction pits and fragments of heath provide some compensation for the losses and are now mananged as a nature reserve.

References

Limber, M. (2011), *Peat Exploitation on Thorne Moors: A case study from the Yorkshire-Lincolnshire border 1626-1963, with integrated notes on Hatfield Moors*, University of Bradford (see www.bradscholars.brad.ac.uk)

Malone, S. and Williams, M. (eds) (2005), *Rumours of Roman Finds: Recent work on Roman Lincolnshire*, Heritage Trust of Lincolnshire

Plaxton, S. and Graham, T. (2015), *Landscape Conservation Action Plan*, Isle of Axholme and Hatfield Chase Landscape Partnership

Robinson, D.N. (2001), *The Book of the Lincolnshire Seaside*, Baron Books, Buckingham

Simmons, I.G. (2015), *The landscape development of the Tofts of south-east Lincolnshire 1100 - 1650*, in Landscape History, Volume 36 Issue 1

Squires, S. (2017), *Ironstone Mining in the Lincolnshire Wolds*, Society for Lincolnshire History & Archaeology

Tonks, E. (1991), *The Ironstone Quarries of the Midlands: History, Operation & Railways – Part VIII South Lincolnshire*, Runpast Publishing

RIGHT: **Bass Maltings, Sleaford**

18 : MODERN LINES
Technology, Development & Defence in the Countryside, 1900 - 2018

We have seen in previous chapters how the Lincolnshire landscape has undergone successive major changes at the hand of man since the Ice Age. Some scientists even refer to the last 2000 years as a new geological epoch, the Anthropocene. With the 20th century, however, we enter an era of unprecedented change affecting all aspects of the Lincolnshire countryside and its people, encompassing both established activities such as agriculture, forestry, quarrying and drainage and new developments such as motor transport, electricity and aviation. Intertwined with these changes are the two World Wars and the Cold War, which have also left their mark in the countryside. Change is still underway today, as new crops and energy technologies continue to modify the rural landscape in the 2010s.

This chapter provides an overview of new lines in the countryside from 1900 to the present, and finds that the period has added its own dramatic, if not always beautiful, contribution to Lincolnshire's multi-layered landscape. Some of these 'modern' lines have themselves passed already into heritage and archaeology, such as disused military airfields and wartime defences.

FACING PAGE: **1970s concrete curve, Covenham Reservoir**

RIGHT: **line of WWII pillboxes built on 1940s coastline, Butterwick**

Roads reborn: petroleum, tarmac and the motorways

We left roads in Chapter 14 at the end of the turnpike era, when the rise of the railways effectively killed off long-distance road transport. By the 1880s, even trunk routes had become quiet and were only used for local journeys (*Barton, 2016). However, the early decades of the 20th century saw a dramatic comeback for roads with the spread of motor vehicles, including the car,

240

bus, coach and lorry. As if to annoint this new era, 'tarmacadam' was discovered accidently in Britain in 1901. Remarkably, virtually all of the nation's roads had been topped using this material by the 1920s as the previous, 'macadamised' surface of compacted stone was unsuitable for mass motor traffic (*Barton, 2016). Ominously for the railways, line closures started in the 1920s and rail would never recover its pre-WWI hegemony in either passenger travel or freight. The interwar years were a time of unprecedented state planning that also saw the introduction of Britain's modern road numbering system (Moran, 2009) and the building of new roads and dual carriageways. Road traffic continued to grow inexorably after WWII with the creation of the motorway network from the 1950s. Another era of bold state planning and spending climaxed symbolically with the opening of the Humber Bridge in 1981, at that time the longest single-span suspension bridge in the world. Thatcher's 'great car economy' saw a vast programme of bypasses and road widening in the 1980s, with the anti-roads backlash growing into a significant political force by the 90s.

Lincolnshire shared in all of these national developments to some degree. Bypasses were built on the A1 at Colsterworth (1926), Stamford (1960), Grantham (1960) and Long Bennington (1968), and the county gained its only stretch of motorway – the M180 and M181 spur – in the 1970s. Subsequently, road construction has focused mainly on further dualling and bypasses on trunk routes such as the A46 and A17, some of which

TOP LEFT: **south cable anchorage, Humber Bridge, Barton-upon-Humber**

LEFT: **A46 Lincoln Bypass**

were environmentally controversial. At Leadenham, bypass protestors occupied woodland on the proposed route in the mid 1990s. At the time of writing, the Lincoln Eastern Bypass is under construction and will dramatically impact the countryside of the city's eastern fringe.

Utilities for the nation: pylons, poles, masts and towers

Electricity transmission lines are now a common feature in the Lincolnshire landscape, arguably having a particularly pronounced visual impact here due to the expansive topography and long vistas. Pylons inevitably have their niche fans in Britain – notably the Pylon Appreciation Society – but have never really been popular with the public. Antipathy stretches back to the 1920s when the Government established the Central Electricity Board to construct and operate a national system of electricity distribution. Between 1928 and 1933, some 4,000 miles of transmission cable and 26,000 pylons were installed to create the National Grid, in what has been described as the largest ever British peacetime construction project. Early opponents of overhead power lines included prominent artistic and literary figures, whom the CEB dubbed "impractical aesthetes", primarily due to the extra cost and inconvenience of undergrounding cables.

Britain's pylons still follow the original 1920s lattice design, though a possible replacement known as the T-pylon was being discussed in 2011.

RIGHT: **Folkingham Water Tower.** An elegant Modern design built in 1983.

Despite changes in energy generation since the 1920s, surface transmission lines and pylons have been an enduring feature of UK power supply and look set to remain so even as the economy decarbonises and renewables increase. Decentralised generation by individual households, farms and businesses has expanded rapidly in the last 10 years but, so far, off-grid or autonomous buildings remain a novelty in the UK and most renewable generation is plugged into the National Grid.

FACING PAGE: **trunk power lines and pylons, Horkstow Wolds**

RIGHT: **Epic Centre, Lincolnshire Showground.** This eco-building incorporates many aspects of sustainable design in its construction and use of resources. Electricity is generated by wind and solar, while the energy-efficient design reduces the need for heating and energy use.

Less controversial but also having a significant visual impact on rural Lincolnshire are numerous lower tension lines with their wooden poles and transformer boxes. Originating as telegraph poles in the late 19th century, these often overlooked features of the landscape now carry both telephone and electricity cables. In the Netherlands, they have been widely undergrounded for landscape conservation reasons, but this is limited in the UK to sensitive locations in protected landscapes.

Electricity generation before the present century was focused heavily on large, centralised power stations, initially coal-fired, with gas increasing in importance in the 1980s. More recently, renewable generation is adding new lines in the Lincolnshire countryside, including wind farms, solar arrays and biomass installations. Biomass crops including willow and miscanthus are also changing the farmed landscape, as is the expansion of oilseed rape for biodiesel. Some of these developments are controversial, with wind farms in particular being vehemently opposed by some people.

Other modern utilities and telecommunications have created their own lines in the landscape, though not all are visible. Distribution networks including gas, water, sewage and fibre-optic cables lie mostly underground, only revealing themselves in occasional installations, like mushrooms above a hidden fungal mycelium. With modern telecommunications, there are no material lines beyond their masts, antennae and satellites, only an increasingly dense but unseen 'fog' of radio and microwave radiation.

Many dwellings were built in the Lincolnshire countryside in the interwar years, fuelled by population growth, the new mobility offered by the car and bus and a vogue for healthier living away from towns and cities. Suburban 'ribbon development' occurred along main roads, as well as individual bungalows in remoter areas, as here at **Leverton Highgate** (FACING PAGE). The Lincolnshire coastline experienced unregulated development including holiday camps, plotland housing and unauthorised 'shanty towns' of homeless famiies. **Anderby Creek** (LEFT) developed as a small beach resort in the 1920s and 30s when plots of land were sold for new houses. Architecturally, Modernist and Art Deco designs were only occasionally used in rural Lincolnshire, as in this 1930s 'streamlined' **office building near Kirton-in-Lindsey** (BOTTOM LEFT), originally built for the Kirton Lindsey Cement Works. Most private housing followed more conservative 'Tudorbethan' styling, and a plain Neo-Georgian design was usual for local authority housing. Plotlanders used a variety of recycled materials and styles for their self-built chalets, occasionally including old railway carriages.

Interwar housing colonises countryside and coast: ribbon development and 'plotlands'

Seen from the present decade, the interwar years of the 1920s and 30s are receding into distant history yet are still recognisably and iconically modern. The period juxtaposed severe social and economic strife with rapid growth and rising prosperity for some. Thus, Hollywood films, Art Deco and the *Mallard* rail speed record sit alongside the General Strike, the Great Depression and the Jarrow March. Personal experience of the period depended much on wealth and location, with the new suburbs and

244

South booming while Northern cities, traditional manufacturing areas and agriculture slumped. Lincolnshire saw both sides of this socio-economic divide. As in much of England, rapid urban growth occurred as 'ribbon development' along the newly-tarmacked arterial roads leading out from the towns, especially Lincoln, as well as in villages close enough to allow daily commuting by car or bus. Most of this housing still exists, variously modified with new windows, doors, roofs and extensions.

Development also occurred in more remote rural locations as part of a growing flight from the cities to escape their smoke, grime and unemployment. This was an era of new smallholdings in the countryside, as well as simply getting away from it all, with the bungalow being the characteristic dwelling type in both cases. Others sought a new life on the Lincolnshire coast in the context of housing shortages and homelessness after WWI. 'Shanty towns' of squatters developed in coastal dunes, with people living in a variey of shacks, ex-army huts, caravans and old railway carriages, often in insanitary conditions. By contrast, most 'plotlanders' leased or purchased land to build their new chalets and holiday cottages.

FACING PAGE: **Humberstone Fitties in 2018.** The Fitties is the best-preserved plotland development on the Lincolnshire coast. The first huts were built in WWI by soldiers billetted in the area to construct Haile Sands Fort. The site then developed as a plotland of dwellings and holiday homes, apart from a return to military use in WWII. Most of the huts have been augmented and upgraded over the decades, but the site retains aspects of the founders' individualism and bohemian approach to life.

In the same period, increasing numbers of campers and caravanners added to the pressures on the coast, threatening to degrade important wildlife habitats. Growing environmental and social concerns led to the Lindsey County Council (Sandhills) Act of 1932, which gave the council extensive powers of protection and acquisition on the Lincolnshire coast between Gibraltar Point and Saltfleet. Unauthorised dwellings were removed and nature reserves established at Rimac and Gibraltar Point. Humberstone Fitties survives as an example of unplanned coastal development, as it lay outside the area covered by the Act and was a lawful plotland which developed from a WWI army camp (Dowling, 2001; Kime, 2005).

National concern about unplanned growth and ribbon development led to a series of partial planning acts in the 1920s and 30s, culminating after WWII in the 1947 Town & Country Planning Act. Thenceforth, housing growth would be contained and focused around towns and in larger service villages. Nevertheless, some housing development in open countryside did occur after 1947 with rows of council houses, especially in the Fens.

Military lines and the legacy of war: runways, radar and coastal defences

Aviation was a new development in the early 20th century that added a novel set of linear features to the landscape, notably airfields and their runways. Not all aviation was related to the military, but this came to dominate in Lincolnshire in terms of its scale and history. Historically, the first use of aircraft for bombing was apparently by Italy in the Turco-Italian

War of 1911 - 12 (Percy & Ryan, 2014). Faced with this novel threat, military aircraft were already operating in Lincolnshire by 1914, with a naval squadron being based near Skegness to patrol the coast. As German bombing raids increased in 1916, a chain of Home Defence 'landing grounds' was established along Britain's east coast by the Royal Flying Corps, the army's air unit, including 6 in Lincolnshire initially. By early 1918, when the Royal Air Force (RAF) was formed, there were 35 military airfields in Lincolnshire (*Bennett & Bennett, 2001). WWI runways were generally of grass, so have left little trace today, though some hangars and related airfield buildings survive, as at Bracebridge Heath.

Several WWI airfields continued in use as active RAF bases after 1918, while others were reopened when hostilities resumed in WWII. Lincolnshire was home to both fighter and bomber squadrons in the latter conflict, but it was the activity of Bomber Command which has become particularly associated with the county – hence the 'Bomber County' label. In addition to the established bases, many new airfields were created and, by April 1945, Lincolnshire had 21 bomber airfields and a force of 700 Lancasters. RAF radar stations were built in several locations, of which the mast at Stenigot has survived and is now a listed structure. After WWII, a majority of the military airfields were decommissioned and returned to farmland. A few saw new commercial uses or residential development. The active bases remained as part of the landscape with ongoing use through

LEFT: **disused concrete taxi-way, former RAF Ingham.** The three runways of this airfield were of grass and have long been returned to farmland.

Britain faced a very real threat of invasion by Hitler's forces in the early stages of WWII, especially prior to the defeat of the Luftwaffe in the Battle of Britain. Extensive defences were put in place along the length of Britain's east coast, especially in Lincolnshire with its low-lying beaches. Today, remains of this 'Coastal Crust' can still be seen, including pill boxes, gun emplacements and anti-tank defences. Further linear defences were located inland, defining 'boxes' that were designed to contain invading forces in the event of a breakout from the coast. Military use of the Lincolnshire coast continued in the Cold War, and RAF coastal bombing ranges remain in use at Theddlethorpe and in the Wash.

RIGHT: **WWII pillbox by The Haven, near Boston**

BOTTOM RIGHT: **1940s *Comet* tank on former RAF bombing range, Theddlethorpe**

249

the Cold War to the present. However, there is also an important military archaeology associated with the disused bases, and concrete taxi-ways can still be found hidden in the coutryside, often reused as access tracks for farm machinery and agricultural storage.

As with airfields, army bases and anti-invasion defences in the countryside span both World Wars and the Cold War. In WWII, anti-invasion defences formed a continous barrier along the Lincolnshire coast named the 'Coastal Crust', which included concrete emplacements for guns, pill boxes, wire, minefields and other anti-landing obstacles. Further linear defences including the strategic GHQ Line were sited inland (Osborne, 2010).

LEFT: **civil air traffic control radar tower, Normanby Top, Wolds**

BOTTOM LEFT: **parabolic dishes, former Stenigot Radar Station**

FACING PAGE: **International Bomber Command Memorial, Canwick Heath, Lincoln**

250

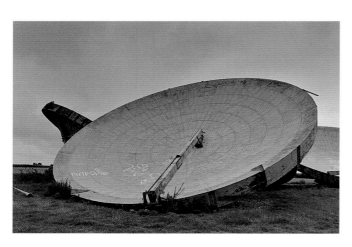

After 1945, the Cold War augmented Lincolnshire's military landscape with new features, including missile launch sites and early warning radar installations. Examples included the geometrically arranged *Bloodhound* missile launchpads at RAF North Coates and the parabolic concrete dishes at Stenigot, built close to the WWII radar tower. With the end of the Cold War in 1991, both these sites have been decommissioned. However, the MOD retains a significant presence in Lincolnshire, including the RAF bases at Coningsby, Cranwell, Scampton and Waddington. The International Bomber Command Memorial at Lincoln is the most recent addition to the county's aviation heritage.

Managing the land: science versus nature?

The 20th century also saw a dramatic intensification in the use of land, with the increasing application of science and technology in agriculture and forestry, often manifested as bold new lines in the countryside.

We noted in Chapter 9 how plantations and 'scientific forestry' became established on country estates by the 19th century. However, a shortage of timber after WWI led to the creation in 1919 of the Forestry Commission (FC) as a state body tasked with increasing woodland. The FC had become the nation's biggest landowner by 1939, with large areas of coniferous forest established from 1920 onwards. In Lincolnshire, activity was focused on the sandy soils of the Coversands, sadly contributing to the loss of semi-natural heathland in the county. Faced with mounting criticism of its blanket conifer planting, FC's approach to landscapes and wildlife has become more sympathetic during the post-WWII period.

Major changes to agriculture began on the eve of WWII, as the horse was replaced by the tractor and, later, the combine harvester. From the 1960s, the use of fertilisers and pesticides went hand in hand with a dramatic

FACING PAGE: **crop covers near Donington, Fens**

RIGHT: **poplar plantation in Brant valley, Vale of Trent.** Many landowners planted poplar stands in the late 1940s and 50s, assured by British matchmakers Bryant & May that there would be a secure market for the timber. In the event, use of matches declined and plastics replaced other uses for poplar veneer. Today, stands of unfelled poplar hybrids remain as a distinctive feature of many lowland valleys in eastern England.

254

shift from mixed farming to intensive arable cropping in eastern counties like Lincolnshire, with the European Common Agricultural Policy adding a further driver for intensification from the 1970s.

Collectively, these changes altered much of the visual vocabulary of the Lincolnshire countryside as it existed before WWII. Many historic lines were lost as field amalgamation led to the widespread removal of hedges and dykes, but new lines appeared too. In the fields, tractor marks became ubiquitous and machine-bailed hay and straw replaced traditional haycocks, stooks and ricks. In the present century, the use of plastics and other materials as crop covers has added further lines, especially in the Fens.

Concerns about the ecological impacts of intensive farming led to better wildlife practices and a further set of linear features on farmland from the 1980s, including replanted hedgerows, tree belts and wildlife or game strips. These have softened the harsh geometry of post-War arable to some extent, though the overall appearance of most of Lincolnshire's farmed landscape remains one of intensive arable production. At the same time, nature conservation bodies have added their own signature to the landscape via nature reserves with ecological management and habitat creation. At the time of writing, the future of UK farming and environmental subsidies is surrounded by uncertainty, but the integration of agriculture and wildlife conservation will hopefully continue as a key aim of future policy.

TOP LEFT: **traditional hay meadow and hedges, Kingerby Beck Meadows**

LEFT: **wildflower strip by arable field, Thorpe-le-Fallows, Vale of Trent**

References

Dowling, A. (2001), *Humberstone Fitties: the Story of a Lincolnshire Plotland*

Hancock, T. (2004), *Bomber County: A History of the Royal Air Force in Lincolnshire*, Midland Publishing

Judson, P. and Lester, C. (eds) (2001), *Twentieth Century - What Heritage?*, Heritage Lincolnshire

Kime, W. (2005), *The Lincolnshire Seaside*, Sutton Publishing, Stroud

Moran, J. (2009), *On Roads: A Hidden History*, Profile Books, London

Osborne, M. (2010), *Defending Lincolnshire: A Military History from Conquest to Cold War*, The History Press, Stroud

Percy, C. and Ryan, N. (2014), *Lincolnshire Aviation in World War I*, Aviation Heritage Lincolnshire

RIGHT: **dawn sunburst in forestry plantation, Tealby Moor, Lindsey Vale**

General References (Note: these references are marked with an asterisk in the text)

Barton, B. (2016), *Civil Engineering Heritage: East Midlands*, Ruddocks

Bates, E. (ed) (2004), *Farming in Lincolnshire 3000 BC to 2000 AD*, Heritage Lincolnshire

Bennett, S. and Bennett, N. (2001), *An Historical Atlas of Lincolnshire*, Phillimore

Crane, N. (2016), *The Making of the British Landscape: From the Ice Age to the Present*, Weidenfeld & Nicolson

Dinnis, R. & Stringer, C. (2013), *Britain: One Million Years of the Human Story*, Natural History Museum, London

Grigg, D. (1966), *The Agricultural Revolution in South Lincolnshire*, Cambridge University Press

Hall, D. and Coles, J. (1994), *Fenland Survey*, English Heritage

Pevsner, N. (second edition, 1989), *The Buildings of England: Lincolnshire*, Yale University Press

Pryor, F. (2010), *The Making of the British Landscape: How We Have Transformed the Land, from Prehistory to Today*, Allen Lane

Pryor, F. (2014), *Home: A Time Traveller's Tales from Britain's Prehistory*, Penguin Books

Thirsk, J. (1957), *English Peasant Farming: The Agrarian History of Lincolnshire from Tudor to Recent Times*, Methuen

Wright, N. (ed) (2004), *Lincolnshire's Industrial Heritage - A Guide*, Society for Lincolnshire History and Archaeology

256

Acknowledgements

Thanks to Adam Daubney, Anne Goldsmith, Michael Knight, Marc Maitland, David Would, Ian Wright and the Humber Keel & Sloop Preservation Society, plus the many others who helped me directly or indirectly in producing this book. Special thanks to Lois for her unwavering support.